THE PRACTICE OF
LOVING
PRESENCE

*A Mindful Guide To
Open-Hearted Relating*

Ron Kurtz
with Donna Martin

STONE'S THROW
PUBLICATIONS

Cover design, Interior Layout and Design: Sue Reynolds,
                                Stone's Throw Publication Services
Cover image: bigstockphoto.com

To contact Donna Martin, please email: psomadonna@gmail.com

ISBN: 978-1-987813-29-6 (paperback book)

Published by Stone's Throw Publication Services
        13240 Mast Road,
        Port Perry, ON   L9L 1B5
        www.stonesthrowps.ca

        1   2   3   4   5   6   7   8   9   10

Earth's the right place for love.
I don't know where it's likely to go better.

~ Robert Frost

TABLE OF CONTENTS

The Legacy of Ron Kurtz   1

Foreword by Flint Sparks   5

Preface by Donna Martin   9

Introduction by Ron Kurtz   11

Discovering Loving Presence   16

What is the state of mind of Loving Presence?   18

How The Practice of Loving Presence Unfolds   25

Mindfulness and Loving Presence   28

Loving Presence is a State of Mind   30

What is Mindfulness?   33

Stages in the practice of Loving Presence   37

THE PRACTICES

Mindfulness Practice   41

Being With   43

Groundlessness   46

Seeing and Being Seen   49

Seeing Through   52

Priming the Pump   55

Search for Inspiration   57

Loving Presence   60

Before You Speak   65

WHERE LOVING PRESENCE IS NEEDED

Where is Loving Presence needed most?   71

With your Life Partner   73

With Children   75

With Friends   83

With Family   85

With the Sick or Dying   87

With Patients or Clients   89

Within a Group   90
Peacemaking   93
Loving Presence with Yourself   98

PRACTICE GUIDE

About these Practices   105
Mindfulness   107
Being With   108
Leaning Toward and Away   109
Monkey Mind   110
Groundlessness   111
Listen Without Deciding   113
Seeing and Being Seen   114
Blink   115
Who Do You See? (A Larger Self)   116
Seeing Through   117
Walking Toward   119
Priming the Pump   121
Search for Inspiration and Nourishment   122
Being With 1-2-3   123
Hand on the Back   124
Intimacy   125
Loving Presence   126
Before You Speak   127

I Take Refuge   128
References/Bibliography   131
About Donna Martin   135

*Real love comes with a powerful recognition
that we are fully alive and whole
despite our wounds or our fears or our loneliness.
It is a state where we allow ourselves to be seen clearly
by ourselves and by others, and in turn,
we offer clear seeing to the world around us.
It is a love that heals.*

~ Sharon Salzberg, "Real Love"

Ron Kurtz (1934 – 2011)

THE LEGACY OF RON KURTZ

RON KURTZ ORIGINATED a mindfulness-based way of doing psychotherapy that has become known as the **Hakomi Method.** He co-founded, with others, the **Hakomi Institute** in the early '80s, and later, in the '90's, he started **Ron Kurtz Trainings** and the **Hakomi Education Network.** He is the author of *Body Centered Psychotherapy: the Hakomi Method,* and *The Body Reveals.*

His background in mathematics, science, and systems theory were the underpinning of his work in designing Hakomi. After completing his graduate training in experimental psychology, Ron taught at San Francisco State College, led encounter groups, and studied Gestalt. He was a client of John Pierrakos, one of the founders of Bioenergetics, and read the works of people like Wilhelm Reich and Alexander Lowen. He describes these experiences as "the beginnings of the Hakomi Method." He was influenced by aspects of Focusing, Ericksonian Hypnosis, and Neuro-Linguistic Programming (NLP), as well as by yoga, Buddhism and Taoism. He also studied with Moshe Feldenkrais and based much of the Hakomi Method on this approach. According to Ron, "These threads: eastern philosophy, psychotherapeutic technique, and systems theory are the foundations of Hakomi."

Hakomi pioneered, among other things, the use of mindfulness as a fundamental ingredient of psychotherapy. Ron realized the need for psychotherapy to be experiential to be truly transformative.

The use of little experiments in mindfulness is key to how Hakomi gently evokes unconscious core memories, experiences and beliefs, especially those that are limiting or cause unnecessary suffering. Bringing these into consciousness where they can be observed and possibly transformed is a gateway to healing change.

Research has confirmed that the most important ingredient in any psychotherapy process (after the client of course), is the therapist's relationship with the client. Ron realized that a good therapeutic alliance depends largely on the personhood and state of mind of the therapist and that this focus must be fundamental in any successful therapy training. Ron recognized that the ideal state of mind for therapists – which can be cultivated with practice – was what he began to call "Loving Presence". This became the foundation of his way of teaching Hakomi to professionals and lay people alike. By the mid '90s Ron's Hakomi trainings were open to anyone who wanted to cultivate those personhood qualities and skills that would help them to be a healing presence for another.

Ron described Hakomi as a method of "mindfulness-based assisted self-study" He continued throughout his life to develop this elegant and highly effective way of bringing healing to the human community. Until his death in 2011, he actively practiced and taught, and continually refined this innovative approach.

All of the organizations created by Ron share a deep appreciation for him as the originator of Hakomi, and for the humor, generosity and love he demonstrated in his trainings. His way of working and teaching was human and playful and deeply compassionate. He moved more and more toward an appreciation of how much the collaboration of practitioner and client (and ideally of a group) could facilitate a nourishing experience of transformation and healing for all the participants in the process.

The foundational principles of Hakomi are Unity, Organicity, Mindfulness, Nonviolence, and Mind/Body wholeness. The foundation of these is loving presence. Ron said, *"Unity reminds us of the interconnectedness of all things, of all life, of all events. It*

Ron and his daughter, Lily

is holism on a universal scale... unity reminds us of the ever bigger picture, of the fact that we are intimately connected with each other, and connected to our culture, our environment, our world... if you ground yourself in the five principles, a particular style and feel and way of being with others will naturally emerge... we don't have to try and learn to be in a state of loving presence. Loving Presence is an attitude that will naturally emerge in us as we come to deeply understand these universal spiritual principles..."

It was Ron's wish that the practice of Loving Presence be made available to as many people as possible. This is the immense contribution to the world that is the legacy of Ron Kurtz.

For one human being to love another,
that is perhaps the most difficult of all our tasks,
the ultimate, the last test and proof
— the work for which all other work
is but preparation.

~ Rainer Maria Rilke

Flint Sparks, Donna Martin & Ron Kurtz

FOREWORD

RON KURTZ WAS A CHARACTER, uniquely gifted and singularly engaging. Once you met him you never forgot him, and once he truly connected with you, he never forgot you either.

This is Ron's book, which he was sadly unable to complete, and it is about this special way in which he was able to meet and influence people. It is both a personal glimpse into who he was, as well a guide to encourage people to meet each other in this same beautiful way. He called this way of meeting Loving Presence and it ultimately came to define the essence of his life's work. It is a map for open-hearted living as well as a series of mindful practices for everyday relationships.

Anyone who had the great blessing of knowing Ron has a story. He loved telling stories, especially if they were funny, and he used them wisely as a master teacher. I think if he had not been a creative innovator in mindfulness and psychotherapy he could have been a comedic entertainer. But at the end of all of our delightful stories about Ron the punch-line is always the same: You loved the guy and you knew he loved you. He somehow left you with a deep knowing that you were someone worth loving and that your love was something worth offering.

Those of us who were privileged to know him often recount our personal stories about Ron, especially now that he is gone, but it is never the content of the stories which lingers. In the end it is the overall feeling invoked by the simple invitation he made with those expressive hands, the warm embrace of his outstretched arms, his wry, knowing smile, and the watery look in his eyes that somehow gently affirmed your being without words.

At the heart of it all is Loving Presence and through these intimate moments with Ron we discovered that this foundational state of mind could transform our lives if we engaged the practices. It was this state of presence, within which all of our old cramped stories about ourselves, our repetitive cycles of suffering, and our hidden fears would begin to fade. By engaging the practices of assisted self-discovery in mindfulness outlined in this book you too can discover that Loving Presence is a key to personal wellbeing and relational freedom.

I first met Ron at Esalen in 1993 during the time when he was beginning to offer the Loving Presence practice sequence apart from the full Hakomi training. As a Clinical Psychologist and psychotherapist, this way of working was revolutionary and inspiring to me. At the same time I was also beginning my formal Zen training at the San Francisco Zen Center and looking for the ways in which these two paths complemented each other. At the end of that first Loving Presence weekend at Esalen, Ron spoke to us about a training he was formulating which would begin the following summer. This was to be a month-long training, held each August over a three-year period. It was an intensive, residential retreat style training which he called "Psychotherapy as Spiritual Practice." Suddenly, what was manifesting before me was an opportunity to enter a remarkable training sequence which integrated psychotherapeutic skills and spiritual practice. This was Hakomi with a difference.

In that three-year training I first met Donna Martin, one of the teachers and staff working alongside Ron. She and I made an instant connection which has deepened over the past 25 years. From the beginning it was clear that she was becoming Ron's most trusted and able co-facilitator and I loved her way of working and simply being in the world. With her background in yoga, Feldenkrais, and mindfulness-based psychotherapy, she was a natural. And, she was someone who could hold her own alongside Ron.

From that training which began in 1994 until his death in 2011, I spent many weeks assisting and teaching with both Ron and Donna. This was a great gift and a treasured time in my life. Through all of this Donna was clearly emerging as his primary successor, especially in the ways in which Ron continued to evolve and practice Hakomi during this final stage in his life. She carried his legacy, along with others of us who Ron acknowledged*, but Donna was clearly his senior disciple. So it is altogether appropriate that Donna has now taken this material and has completed this lovely volume as a tribute to Ron's masterful innovations in the Loving Presence training. Her love for the work and her own magnificent presence shine through on every page.

If you follow the path that Ron laid out in the Loving Presence sequence and use the guideposts and practices which Donna so clearly outlines here, you will walk with them into the spacious field of Loving Presence.

The Buddha was quite clear in his teachings that awakening and the relief of unnecessary suffering was something which unfolds in the intimate space between people and among all things. No one person can do it alone. The great Jewish philosopher Martin Buber,

* The Legacy Holders in alphabetical order: Jeff Chernove, Adama Hamilton, Donna Martin, Georgia Marvin, Bob Milone, Pat Ogden, Flint Sparks.

in describing the transformative power of the I-Thou relationship famously stated, "All real living is meeting." The English novelist and essayist E. M. Forster guides us in this same direction in his succinct statement, "Only connect!" Rainer Maria Rilke wrote in his advice to a young poet, "For one human being to love another human being: that is perhaps the most difficult task that has been entrusted to us, the ultimate task, the final test and proof, the work for which all other work is merely preparation."

In the end, Ron was clear that Loving Presence was the essential work for which all other work is merely preparation. Enjoy this manual and prepare yourself well. Softening barriers to love will reveal a way to live joyfully and intimately, to connect generously and honestly.

This is the path of Loving Presence.

~ Flint Sparks

Ron Kurtz and Donna Martin

PREFACE

I MET RON KURTZ, THE CREATOR OF HAKOMI, in 1990 at Hollyhock, a wonderful retreat center on Cortes Island in western Canada where I have taught yoga and other things for many years.

I had heard he was coming, so a few months before the workshop I read his book, *BodyCentered Psychotherapy: the Hakomi Method.* I was powerfully touched and remember thinking, "this [Hakomi] sounds like what I do, what I am trying to do!"

Ron was there for about a week with his wife Terry and their baby daughter Lily. We had a beautiful connection that summer followed by my joining a Hakomi training with him in Portland Oregon. We even taught some workshops together right away, on Yoga and Hakomi.

Soon after I began teaching with Ron, he had the inspiration for the **Practice of Loving Presence,** which has become foundational in how we now teach the Hakomi Method. Not only did Ron recognize the power and significance of this state of mind for therapists, as well as for anyone in any kind of significant relationship, but he was able to brilliantly articulate a sequence of stages we can move through to cultivate this way of being. He also created a series of very simple but powerful Hakomi practices for each stage.

We began to teach this practice of Loving Presence in the mid '90s, first to Hakomi students in our trainings, and then in weekend workshops to anyone who was interested. Soon we realized that we could complement and enhance the practice with a focus on three other key themes related to Loving Presence: quieting the mind, nonverbal communication, and emotional nourishment. We developed practices around these themes. The poetic titles of these are:

- *Inner Silence: Quieting the Mind*
- *Wisdom without Words: Nonverbal Communication*
- *Emotional Nourishment: the Art of Comforting*

We taught these practices in groups all over the world until Ron's death in 2011 and I (and others) have continued to teach these as fundamental to learning Hakomi. They are not only relevant to anyone in a helping profession or in any helping role, but to all who aspire to relate to others with more consciousness and compassion.

A few years ago, while reading David Crow's *In Search of the Medicine Buddha,* I saw this little prose poem he wrote and realized that it both perfectly sums up these themes and points to how important they are for any kind of healing to happen.

> *Wisdom without words*
> *Born of inner silence*
> *Carried within the heart*
> *Dispensed with loving kindness*
> *This is true medicine.*

The book you have in your hands here offers the heart of the approach, the practice of Loving Presence. This is intended as a practice guide to an open hearted state of mind and way of relating. The practices are based on the Hakomi way of using simple self-study experiences in mindfulness to cultivate relational habits that can produce healing results from any human interaction. In my opinion, this is the greatest legacy of Ron Kurtz and his version of Hakomi.   *~ Donna Martin*

Introduction by
Ron Kurtz

The Practice of Loving Presence

ONE OF MY TEACHERS TOLD ME I was 'good with people'. So, I thought about that. What does that mean? Well, I think it means that people feel better after being with me, especially if they've come with some kind of distress. Yes, I think that's what it means. It could also mean I'm a good manipulator, that I'm skillful in 'handling' people, 'difficult' people. It could mean that kind of skill. Or it could mean that I'm a good teacher, or speaker, or that I'm a good salesman or politician, or all of these. But I want to believe my teacher meant the first one; that people feel better after being with me. That's the one I feel best about.

Well, I thought, I'm a psychotherapist; I ought to be good with people. I've got a lot of experience with people in distress. Then I asked, what did all that experience teach me? I wasn't always good with people. What is it that I learned that helps me to be good with people now? And what exactly does it mean to be good with people? That's what I want to talk to you about.

Here's what I think it means: when people feel better, they feel better about who they are and what's possible for them. Meher Baba, an Indian spiritual teacher, said, "I can love you better than you can love yourself." I think one way we can be good with or for people is that we feel good about *them*. That's the basis—the real basis—for their beginning to feel good about themselves.

Whatever else we do, we must first of all learn how to like people, or if we can, to love them. I learned a lot about how to do that. I learned to look for and usually find something in each person that I can like, admire, appreciate and even love. I learned to spend my initial time with the person doing this and to ignore a lot of other stuff. After I've found that, my relationship with the person is built on this emotional base. My actions and words very naturally support the person to feel better about himself. It's effortless.

It's different from listening to the person's story and looking for problems to solve. It's looking for what's good and right about the person, not what's wrong. This is not about solving someone's problems. It's not about being a psychotherapist, a medical doctor, a teacher, a lawyer, a manager, a financial advisor or a bus driver. It's not about any of that. It's about being good with people. In any of those professions, you may be very good at solving people's problems and still not be very good with people at all.

Anytime a story is told, there are two more stories in the background. Beyond the story that the storyteller is telling—which is only the words—there's the story of the storyteller's intentions, conscious or not so conscious. In order to get this background story, we must sense it, often through very subtle clues. (Sometimes, not so subtle.) The second background story is the story of the storyteller's history, the experiences that created this way of being. The intentions and the history, though background, are always present. It cannot be otherwise. Both exist before the storyteller even speaks. Both are embedded in the way the story is told and in the teller's way of being.

To be really good with people, we must be good at unfolding the embedded stories of storytellers. You must be interested and motivated to understand people through this unfolding process. It is helpful to be willing and able to withstand the emotional buffeting that sometimes comes with powerful stories of intense experiences. Focus on the storyteller to see through what's being said to the soul of the person saying it. Keeping your distance from the details and complications of the narrative and any abstract questions posed becomes important, as does staying awake to hear the stories embedded of the one within—the one who has been waiting for a listener like you, whether such a listener was ever expected or not.

So, the first thing is liking people, which means having the habit of finding something to like and enjoy with each person you relate to. It's a habit you can cultivate. There are a million ways to do it. I remember that on the day that my infant daughter died in my arms, as I was being driven home, looking out the window of the car at people going about their seemingly much more normal lives, I had the thought, "Everyone was some mother's child." I meant that everyone once felt a mother's love and that love was the greatest experience of our lives. And that though we all share the fact of that experience, we may never once have spoken of it. Remembering this fact about people is one way that I cultivate the habit of liking people.

To be good with people, we need what I would call a *spacious* attitude. We need an openness to being with, to spending time, to giving one's attention to another. We need a willingness to loosen one's attachments to agendas and outcomes. We need to be able to be comfortable in uncertain and undirected situations. If we're too attached to controlling our worlds, we will not be good with people.

Perhaps you can see a connection here between a spacious attitude and the practice of meditation. In meditation, we have "no intention of controlling what happens next", says Stephen Batchelor, in his book, *Buddhism without Beliefs.* Or, we can see a connection to the perennial teachings about happiness. We are happiest when we are serving others and not addicted to self-centered cravings. For this, particular combinations of qualities need to be cultivated. In the Buddhist tradition, the terms are wisdom and compassion: more simply, warmth and wakefulness.

Carl Rogers once did a very significant experiment. He trained secretaries to do "Rogerian therapy." The result was that, on average, the secretaries did better than the trained psychotherapists! This was a very surprising outcome. Because Rogers chose secretaries who had very warm personalities, the clients in those experiments reported that they were more satisfied with their interactions with the secretaries than with the professional therapists. (The clients didn't know that they were secretaries, by the way).

In *Human Change Processes,* Michael Mahoney reported research that showed that the personhood of the therapist was eight times more important that any particular method or technique. In *The Heart and Soul of Change: What Works in Therapy* (Hubble, Duncan, & Miller, 1999). there is a report on page 96 about a study done by Strupp and Hadley, in 1979, which found that "experienced therapists were no more helpful than a group of untrained college professors selected for their relationship skills... it looks as though differences in personal qualities make some therapists more helpful."

These are qualities that anyone can cultivate. I want to emphasize that anyone can learn these things. That is what I want you to know: that we can all be good with people, good with each other. The Practice of Loving Presence is a guide to exactly this.

By the mid '90s I began emphasizing Loving Presence as the appropriate state of mind for a practitioner or healing assistant to hold in any therapeutic process. I was clear that this way of supporting another person was the first and most important task if we are to be of help in the process of therapeutic self-discovery. The identification of this state of mind as essential to healing and transformational relationships was not entirely novel, but the idea that a person can be trained, through a carefully crafted sequence of experiential exercises, to cultivate this loving container, was a unique and creative addition to the work. This one change made an enormous difference in the effectiveness of Hakomi and has become the foundation of the method.

Hakomi rests on a strong scientific foundation, with a deep background in Eastern wisdom traditions. Loving Presence represents the heart of Hakomi, and is cultivated through a well-developed sequence of experiential practices.

Here's how it first came to me...

Discovering Loving Presence

IN MY TRAININGS, I WOULD OFTEN DEMONSTRATE HAKOMI in front of the class by working with one person after another, often using a translator when in other countries. The idea of Loving Presence occurred to me during one such training.

Doing several sessions every day, after a few days I became exhausted and began to lose my concentration. While I was working with one man in front of the group, I slowly realized I had lost the thread of his story and had no idea what was happening for him or what to do. I decided to go on as if nothing was amiss and hope that my head would clear.

So I simply continued to look at him. His eyes were closed and he kept on talking, not realizing that I had no idea what he was talking about. I waited and hoped that when it was time to respond to him, I would think of something to say.

As I looked at him with no other agenda but to wait, I found myself fascinated by his face. He began to look really beautiful to me. It was like looking at a masterpiece of art, a Vermeer or a Van Gogh. I think this was the result of my decision to simply relax and let myself be empty-headed.

I began to feel moved by the visual beauty of his face. At first, it was all about composition, colors, shades and highlights. Purely visual. As I continued, it slowly changed to include more about him. Gradually I became aware of something deep and immensely powerful. We could call it his humanity, his **human beingness.** I began to feel a deep love and compassion for him. He was not a particularly striking man. He was actually quite ordinary. It was more about his spirit, his aliveness.

Here was a fellow human being, a fellow creature. I saw that his suffering was my suffering. It was all our suffering. I felt great compassion for him and for all living beings. I also realized that this wonderful feeling I was having was probably the most important part of our relationship—of any relationship in fact—and that, with his eyes closed, he was not the least bit aware of it.

When some people are being mindful or go deeply within themselves, they tend to close their eyes. I wanted him to know how I was feeling; that seemed important to me. So, when it was appropriate, I interrupted his talking and asked him to open his eyes and to look at me while he talked.

Up to then, his talking wasn't very significant, just the usual "this happened and that happened". When he opened his eyes and looked at me, he could see the compassion and love I was feeling and he began to respond to that immediately. His deeper feelings came to the surface. His process moved into real issues. As he became more real, I felt even more love and compassion for him. Our connection became more and more intimate. His feelings became stronger and everyone present was moved by them. And so it went, moment by moment, more and more real, more and more healing. The outcome was very nourishing for all of us.

So, I discovered something really important. I discovered the power of simply being present and allowing my heart to open. I learned about the cycle of compassion and opening. From that moment on, Loving Presence became the foundation of my work – of the way I practice and teach Hakomi. It can be said that when the mind is quiet, the heart will do the work.

What is the state of mind of Loving Presence?

LOVING PRESENCE IS EASY TO RECOGNIZE when it's happening. Imagine a happy and contented parent looking at the sweet face of their peaceful newborn baby. The parent is calm, loving, and attentive. Unhurried and undistracted, the two of them seem to be outside of time... simply being rather than doing. And, gently held within a field of love and life's wisdom, they are as present with each other as any two persons could be. This is the picture of what I mean by Loving Presence.

When someone offers Loving Presence in a relationship, the other—perhaps without even realizing it—feels safer, witnessed, appreciated, and even understood. And the person offering loving presence feels calm, spacious, and focused. This is true in any kind of relationship. It is especially true when one person has the intention to be helpful to the other, whether this helping role is personal or professional.

So how do we do it?

In Loving Presence, we give a high priority to being present and compassionate, both with ourselves and with the person we are with, at the same time. We set aside task-oriented agendas of advising or fixing or figuring out what's wrong, because when we get too busy looking for problems to solve, it becomes impossible to develop or sustain Loving Presence.

Loving Presence is a practice of shifting our attention toward a feeling of appreciation with the intention of simply being with another, human to human. It requires as a first step that we learn about our own habits and automatic tendencies, and decide whether they support or interfere with being present in this way. These might be habits of making assumptions, focusing on what's wrong, overanalyzing, wanting or needing to fix, being impatient or busy trying to make something happen. Interrupting these habits and impulses to create a more spacious way of relating is essential to this practice. So this is the second step in the practice—interrupting old habits and creating new space.

The third step is practicing a new way of seeing and perceiving the other. We call it **seeing through**. It's a kind of perceptual wisdom in which we have the intention to see something deeper about the person, beneath the surface and behind the obvious.

It leads naturally to the fourth step, which is finding nourishment in something we see. This involves a search for beauty or inspiration in the other, a recognition of what's right, a willingness to be nourished in a way that has nothing to do with our own worth or abilities, but with a kind of awe about the person and our shared humanity.

When this happens, the last step—the state of Loving Presence—emerges spontaneously. Now we simply enjoy it and let it show in our expression and demeanor.

The practice of Loving Presence teaches about this state of mind, how to cultivate it and how to sustain it. In a simple step-by-step process, you can learn the practice, the stages, the tools, the state of mind, and how to recognize when you're getting in your own way.

The practice of Loving Presence is great for therapists but it is really for anyone. Learning even a little bit of this approach will make all of us more skillfully helpful, with our own and with others' suffering. We can be helpful as friends or teachers, as parents or partners, as well as helping professionals. We are all potential healers, especially when we learn to cultivate this state of mind we are calling Loving Presence.

> *"The simple act of being completely present to another person is truly an act of love; no drama is required."*
>
> ~ Sharon Salzberg

Loving Presence is, first of all, about **being present in the present.** It's about showing up to be all there, ready and able to experience fully. It involves focusing widely, noticing more, for example, than just the verbal content of a conversation. It means recognizing our perceptual habits and opening to new ways of seeing.

Loving Presence requires putting aside our preconceived ideas about someone, and even assumptions we may have about people in general. It means dropping agendas, plans, or routine behaviors that interrupt or constrict the flow of experience in the moment. Loving presence asks us to surrender to the natural unfolding of a relationship, to its mysterious and spontaneous processes.

In his book, ***Phantoms in the Brain***, V. S. Ramachandran tells of a study where people were shown words and images about violence and hostility. Then they looked at pictures of faces, and —thinking it was a separate test—wrote down their impressions. Another group also looked at the same faces and wrote their impressions. The first group saw the faces as threatening and hostile, far more so than anyone in the second group.

It is easy to demonstrate to yourself that your perception is altered by your state of mind. Sit in a public place, for example and take a moment to imagine this fantasy: imagine that everyone you see has saved someone's life. Then notice the qualities that begin to shine in them for you, qualities of courage and kindness, even dignity, for example. Ordinariness and greatness all rolled up in one being? Enjoy the images and perceptions that come with this.

Now imagine that all the adults around you are really only five years old. Imagine that this is a kindergarten setting—have a good look around again. Can you see the child in everyone? The innocence, the vulnerability? It's pretty easy, isn't it?

> *The loveliness is everywhere...*
> *it rises in its own reality*
> *and what we must learn is*
> *how to receive it*
> *into ours.*
>
> ~ Kenneth White

So when we are offering someone our emotional support, what is most important is that we are simply being present in a caring way, and, paradoxically, that we have the intention to search for inspiration in something about the other person. This inspiration becomes so nourishing for us that it sustains us in our ability to stay present in a helpful way—loving presence sustains the energy of the helper.

Giving priority to being inspired and nourished by someone we are helping might seem like a radical idea for those of us who want to be of service. We aren't used to simply finding pleasure in being with someone, especially someone in distress. Whether as helpful friends or as professional therapists, we tend to get too busy with problem-solving, asking questions, or offering advice. But to be in loving presence, we want to avoid being preoccupied with such activities.

The challenge is to drop these kinds of pursuits. Fixing people, solving their problems, having answers to their questions, rescuing, or changing them can all be ways to avoid fear, to feel safe, to have a sense of control, or just to feel good about ourselves. However, in practicing Loving Presence, we want to focus simply on letting ourselves be inspired by the other and then translating that inspiration into compassion, patience, understanding, and constant, loving attention. This takes practice.

> *"Those who are unhappy have no need for*
> *anything in this world but people capable of*
> *giving them their attention.*
> *The capacity to give one's attention to a*
> *sufferer is a very rare and difficult thing;*
> *it is almost a miracle; it is a miracle."*
>
> ~ Simone Weil

How do we find this kind of pleasure in simply being with someone, even when they are suffering? Well, the real question is how do we not find pleasure? What's getting in the way of enjoying ourselves? What's disturbing our capacity for finding pleasure in being with others, especially if being with people is part of our work?

To find pleasure in any relationship situation, it is helpful to be able to stay calm. Staying calm makes us more sensitive, more able to attend to subtle sensations. For this sensitivity we want to let go of trying to achieve anything.

Trying to make something happen, straining, and pushing are not helpful in this process. We have to be very honest with ourselves about our own pride, our need for approval or recognition, or for perfection. Instead we want to slow down enough to take pleasure in whatever happens with whomever is there with us.

And what kind of pleasure do we find? In Loving Presence we move past our ego-based needs and toward a more generous experience of pleasure, a deeply spiritual kind of nourishment. The kind of pleasure we might get out of assisting anyone is the pleasure of offering comfort, of feeling connected, the pleasure of seeing deeply, being real, of understanding and helping someone else understand, helping someone become more alive and more free.

The first thing to explore is how our self-image gets in the way. The kind of pleasure and nourishment we're talking about here is not about feeling good about ourselves. It's not at all ego-centered. It is about being nourished by something about the other person's humanity.

> *"The first part of emotional healing*
> *is being limbically known –*
> *having someone with a keen ear*
> *catch your melodic essence."*
> ~ from *A General Theory of Love*

Whether as helpful friends or as teachers or parents, or even as therapists, being nourished in this way might be all we have to do to give someone the emotional support they need. If we tend to work too hard, we may miss the opportunity to simply let ourselves be nourished, to find pleasure in simply being with someone. If we're too focused on what we think should happen, and on doing something to make it happen, this focus on doing can draw us away from being in Loving Presence. Instead, we want to find a way to appreciate this person and the opportunity to be with them. When we can do this, they often naturally begin to open up right in front of us; a kind of mutual openness and healing begins to happen in a natural way. Being open, our own perceptions and understandings deepen. Only in this kind of intimate connection with another person can we receive the energy and spiritual nourishment we need to sustain Loving Presence.

In this Loving Presence state of mind, the possibility of true understanding is greatly enhanced. We begin to see beneath the surface to the depths of the person we are with. We might see something essential, and beautiful, even divine. We begin to have an intimate connection with the person's essential self.

Out of this growing intimacy, a new attunement and rapport emerges. The outer signs of someone in Loving Presence (being calm, loving eyes, relaxed posture, steady attention) can be seen and felt by the other person. Recognizing this and sensing that this moment is somehow special, the other person begins to relax and perhaps to open a little more. This opening further inspires and nourishes the one in Loving Presence. In this way, Loving Presence inspires the possibility of an emotionally healing and nourishing experience for both. This in turn inspires more Loving Presence. Each sustains the other, one person moving towards deeper caring and compassion, the other towards opening and healing.

> *"In a way, all successful psychotherapy*
> *depends on the ability to detach attention*
> *from habits and to describe them*
> *from the point of view of a neutral observer."*
>
> ~ Helen Palmer

The ultimate goal of being in any kind of therapy is finding freedom from unnecessary suffering. In Hakomi, we assist others in reaching that goal through inviting a commitment to self-study and authenticity. The basis for this kind of self study is a particular way of using mindfulness. By studying oneself in mindfulness, it is possible to discover the inner structures of mind that are causing suffering or at least limiting us in some way, limiting our access to nourishment. This kind of self reflection is also the first step in the practice of Loving Presence.

How The Practice
of Loving Presence Unfolds

AS THE SEQUENCE OF STEPS IN THIS PRACTICE of Loving Presence unfolds, we first want to become aware, in a gentle way, of some of our habitual attitudes and ideas around being in relationship. We use mindfulness, which is that kind of quiet attention to whatever our present experience is and to how we are experiencing it. We use it for self-study so we can notice our own habits, and discover what we tend to do automatically and habitually. We then want to practice relaxing our attachments to these ideas and habits and begin to open up a space for something new.

So the first step is noticing our old habits: habits of perceiving, habits of reacting, habits of making meaning. We want to pay attention to how we are habitually organizing our experience of being with others.

After turning our attention to our habitual states of mind and ways of being, we want to begin to create more space. We want to clear away some of the attitudes and tendencies that obscure clear perception. In this new state of spacious mind, we learn to look and see others more openly, more intuitively, and more appreciatively. We have space now for something new to happen. We begin to see differently, to have new perceptions and impressions.

There is a basic freedom that comes from relaxing our attachments to who we think we are and how things should be. There is a lightness of being, a sense of peace, a spaciousness that makes more room for compassion and intimacy. Relaxation and spaciousness give us an opportunity to establish a whole new level of sensitivity toward others. This spacious mind is about celebrating mystery; it's a way of being that goes beyond the limits of the ordinary.

One aspect of this spaciousness is the ability to see deeply, to see through, to see things with a wide-angle lens and from many different angles. We learn that we can act without controlling. We let go of being attached to particular outcomes. We are more sensitive and open, lowering the noise of internal chatter and the preconceived ideas that interfere with clarity, insight, and intuition. This sensitivity leads to true acceptance and understanding.

As this happens, we begin to experience a pleasant, relaxed, present-centered, open-hearted state of mind.

> *"The loving eye sees through and*
> *beyond image and effects the deepest change."*
> ~ John O'Donohue

Next we create the intention to see something in the other person that inspires us. We very specifically invite and search for qualities in the other that will nourish us—qualities like the person's courage, vulnerability, sensitivity, gentleness, determination, or intelligence. The natural result of finding this—something that inspires and nourishes us—is that we are touched and reminded of the person's natural strengths and innate beauty. Our hearts open simply to see others in their wholeness. Amazingly, the other might realize, perhaps unconsciously, that they are safe to be themselves with us. They feel accepted and appreciated.

From mindfulness, to spaciousness, we begin to see more clearly, and to open to new possibilities of how to be filled up by this experience, how to let this very moment—just as it is—nourish us. This kind of **nourishment** fills us up and then begins to radiate out effortlessly as Loving Presence, providing the ground and context for an emotionally-attuned relationship to unfold spontaneously.

As a final step, we practice **responding** to each other from this state. A flow of Loving Presence and healing is soon established in this way. This reciprocal flow of appreciation becomes the new context for relationship, and the potential for emotional nourishment and even healing is greatly enhanced.

The practices we're offering here are designed to provide ways to help you enter this cycle and sustain it. By following this sequence of steps you can learn to recognize your automatic thoughts and habitual states of mind, and to notice when and how you're getting in your own way, or in the way of whatever healing process wants to happen.

It always comes back to knowing who you are and how you're being. You need first and foremost to be able to recognize and interrupt the habits that get in the way of this state of mind we are calling Loving Presence. For this we recommend a regular practice of mindfulness. You want to become aware of habitual ways of thinking, of feeling, of your habitual expressions and postural habits, of impulses and tendencies, of whatever is on automatic.

How can you learn to be with someone in this way so that you both move together into a loving place where healing can simply unfold spontaneously?

Mindfulness and Loving Presence

EASTERN PHILOSOPHY TEACHES that when the mind becomes silent, a direct experience of spirit emerges. That signal, like the stars that appear when the sun goes down, is really always present. But it is hidden by the noise we are making. And the biggest noise is the clamoring of the mind. Mindfulness, which involves attending to the mind with compassion and without judgement, lowers this noise. When the noise is lowered, whatever signal is being masked can emerge. It seems to appear as if out of a fog.

In the Practice of Loving Presence, we use mindful awareness first of all to focus on our own present experience and to discover the habits and beliefs that inform and organize it. Present experience is a very clear example of how we habitually organize our experience, sometimes in ways that interfere with our intentions.

In this Hakomi approach to self awareness, mindfulness is not just a technique. Mindfulness is a way of surrendering. It involves a deliberate choice to be vulnerable, an intentional sensitivity. As such it is best entered into in a place where we feel safe, and with people whom we trust. Mindfulness is undefended consciousness.

Going into a state of mindfulness as a deliberate choice is not always easy. If we allow ourselves to feel painful emotions in this process, it is because we believe it will be worth it in order to understand ourselves and to heal. From a systems point of view, mindfulness can be understood as a method of making the system more sensitive. By calming down and quieting the mind, we lower the usual noise. Turning inward and focusing on our present experience in the moment enhances our capacity to pick up even our most subtle sensations, feelings, thoughts, images, and significant memories.

Being mindful means deliberately bringing ourselves into this sensitive and vulnerable state. If we're mindful, if our attention is open and simply noticing, even a simple statement or action can evoke quite a deep experience. When we are in mindfulness and experiences are evoked, there is no confusion about the source. We are clear that whatever emerges is our own. We know that any emotional reactions are arising from our own beliefs and history, not imposed by someone else's guesses or assumptions.

Mindfulness is not as easy as it sounds. But when we can do it, there is a possibility of changing what we can experience, what is and is not possible for us, in relationship and in life. It is an essential state of mind to cultivate for the practice of Loving Presence, which is an enhanced state of mindful awareness. It is a state of being radically present in a receptively appreciative way.

Loving Presence is a State of Mind

THERE IS A BASIC FREEDOM THAT COMES from relaxing our attachments to who we think we are and how things should be. There is a lightness of being, a new peacefulness and a feeling of spaciousness that makes room for humor and compassion.

Being in this calm, clear, loving state of mind is not just something we do to be better friends or parents or therapists. It is a spiritual practice, a path to liberation. It creates a sacred space in which both the person suffering and the helper or support person are nourished. This space is the heart of healing.

This spacious mind is about celebrating mystery and humor and a Self beyond the limits of the ordinary ego. It involves acting without always needing to control events or being attached to particular outcomes. We become more sensitive and open.

If we consider very fine distinctions, there are an infinite number of possible states of mind. In practical terms, we learn to live within a limited set, which become highly stable and familiar to us. As we move through our daily lives, we pass from one of these habitual states of mind to another, as the situation changes from sleep to wakefulness, from resting to activity, from one task to another, one social situation to another. Some types of events are triggers for particular states of mind. Some of our habits also have a strong effect on our states of mind.

For example, someone steps on your toes. Depending on who it is, where you are, what you're feeling at the moment, different states of mind could be triggered. If you're happy, at a party, and some good friend of yours accidentally steps gently on your work boot, you're not going to get too upset. But, if you're unhappy about something and a person whom you've never liked steps on your bare toes just as they start confronting you, that might fire off your amygdala, mobilize a lot of muscle tension in your jaw, neck, shoulders and arms, contract your peripheral blood vessels, making you grimace and say something unkind to the person. It all depends.

If you are in the habit of being tolerant and kind, you might not react very much to someone stepping on your toes. If you have a long history of uncontrolled violent outbursts, you might hit them. It all depends on what kind of mental "music" you're in the habit of playing. The way you're organized, the states of mind you've practiced and used a lot, the various components of the brain you habitually recruit, the thoughts and impulses that come easily to mind—these will all determine what happens.

The habitual states of mind of Buddhist monks are different from those of career criminals (though either can change). The poverty-stricken children of the Third World have different states of mind from the rich children of highly industrial countries. They have different memories and habits of thought. Different hopes, ideas, values... different states of mind. They're organized differently.

A good analogy for shifting through different states of mind could be the ways an orchestra changes from one passage of music to another. For various passages in the music, some instruments are playing, others are not. When something loud and dramatic is required, drums and horns are more likely to be playing. For something soft and ethereal, a harp maybe and a flute. For jazz, you want saxophones and pianos. For bluegrass, banjos, mandolins and guitars. Each "state" of the music is played by a different combination of instruments. From the perspective of an individual instrument—a flute, for instance—it might join with the violins for one part of the music and the horns for another. Any individual instrument might be part of any passage, but need not be.

So it is with states of mind. Each state of mind requires its own combination of functional units of the brain. It depends on what "music" is playing. It depends on the entire complex dynamics of internal and external situations. The external situation, the internal biochemical situation, perceptions, the emotions aroused, memories activated, needs felt, thoughts flowing through the mix, and all kinds of habits, biases, modulators and who knows what all. Each state of mind is only one of the many ways to configure the brain. Each is a different kind of mind.

There is an exception to this analogy, however—no external maestro is conducting the brain. The brain is a self-organizing system. There is the possibility that it will self-organize a state of mind in which information from all other systems flows through one component which in turn influences the overall functioning of the whole. The right orbitofrontal cortex of the brain is thought to be where that function is located. For more, see The *Developing Mind* by Dr. Daniel Siegel.

What is Mindfulness?

MINDFULNESS IS A TRADITIONAL METHOD of spiritual practice. In distancing ourselves from all that creates our everyday habitual self, we begin to recognize the Self that does not change, the powerful and universal Self that permeates all.

In mindfulness we are not just having an experience, and notions about our experience, but we are even noticing our notions. It has been defined by Nayanaponika as:

> *"the clear and singleminded awareness of what actually happens to us and in us at the successive moments of perception."*

And by Varela as

> *"A turning of the direction of attention from the exterior to the interior. And a change in the quality of attention, which passes from the looking-for to the letting-come."*

In the **Feeling Buddha,** David Brazier says this about mindfulness:

> *"...mindfulness is to live in the present moment. A freshness of perception is possible to us that most people only rarely experience. Enhanced awareness of the immediate natural environment is a very powerful healing influence upon the wounded psyche. To gaze at the setting sun, to touch a flower, really to hear the birds sing or to feel the weight of a*

stone in your hand is to come in contact with reality in a way that little else can match. In such perfect moments, we are fulfilling our purpose in being here.

Mindfulness is that state of consciousness in which we turn our attention to the flow of our experience, with the added and unusual condition that we have no intention to control what happens. For most people, this is not our usual state of mind. Here are some characteristics of this state called mindfulness:

- In mindfulness, we are not reacting. We are simply noticing our impulses to react. We are noticing the thoughts and experiences that arise moment to moment.

- We are participating as an observer – a silent witness of our own behavior.

- We are at least one step removed from anything that seems to happen by itself in our experience. We have taken a step back.

- We are cultivating that part of the mind that can simply witness, without taking action, and without preferences, whatever experiences arise, including body sensations, emotions, impulses, thoughts or memories.

In Hakomi, we use mindfulness as the basis for studying the underlying habits and ideas that organize our experiences. Since most of what we do and feel and think is habitual, these habits are very close to our sense of who we are. These organizing habits are expressions of the images, beliefs and assumptions we hold about the kind of world we live in as well as who we need to be to live in it safely and to have our needs met.

"The way is easy for one with no preferences."
~Zen saying

To have any choice about the kinds of experiences we can have, we want to discover and study the habits and ideas that are organizing our perceptions and reactions and therefore our experiences.

Research tells us that "much of what we want to know about ourselves resides outside of conscious awareness." So, if we want anything to change, if we want to be able to choose our state of mind, we must first become more aware of ourselves and our habitual states. This is much easier to do with help, and the first thing we want to do in order to assist each other is practice mindfulness together.

> *"Sitting quietly and listening carefully*
> *to yourself, you can observe*
> *the main voice in which*
> *your thoughts recite themselves."*
> ~Robert Thurman

To act mindfully means to remember to enjoy the simple things that we do. To enjoy walking enriches our lives greatly since— unless we have serious health problems—we all spend some time walking. Take my hand and we will walk together. We will look at flowers and smile at passersby. Our walking will be like a beautiful song, a melody that flows on without haste. The point is not to get somewhere. The point is to enjoy something lovely and satisfying. If we do so, then we are fulfilling a higher purpose.

Mindfulness both asks for and results in a kind of spaciousness which means we are lowering the noise of the internal chatter and preconceived ideas that generally interfere with having more clarity, insight, intuition, true acceptance and understanding. In relationship, it creates the possibility of being really good with people.

There are many definitions, and characteristics, of mindfulness, but they all point to a quality of non-judgmental observation. Mindfulness is not "thinking about" something. It is not analytical nor is it a form of concentration. In many ways, it is the open space in which awareness arises.

In the Practice of Loving Presence, since our first intention is self-discovery, we do this through the practice of mindfulness and keeping an experimental attitude, which allows us to attend to moments of our present experience without judgment or bias. In this process we become increasingly skilled at noting what is automatic or habitual.

In mindfulness, there is no intention to control what happens next. That's why it's not so simple. It is a deliberate relinquishing of control. As a skill, mindfulness improves with practice.

The first focus in traditional practice is often on the breath, on simply paying attention to the movements of our own breathing, without interfering. To pay attention to our breath and not control it is more difficult than we might imagine, especially when we think about how little attention we ordinarily pay to our breathing and how well it works outside of our conscious control.

Being relaxed helps to cultivate this quiet state—what meditation teachers call "choiceless awareness." In mindfulness, we allow our mind to become quiet and calm, our breath, our body sensations, our emotions and our thoughts to simply be observed. We focus inward on the flow of our experience.

This is the first stage in the Practice of Loving Presence.

Stages in the Practice of Loving Presence

THE PRACTICES WE ARE OFFERING IN THIS BOOK are organized according to the various stages we want to move through in order to create the conditions where this state of mind we call Loving Presence can emerge effortlessly and spontaneously. They are:

1. Mindfulness and self-study,
2. Relaxation and spaciousness,
3. Perceptual wisdom and sensitivity,
4. Inspiration and nourishment,
5. The state of Loving Presence—allowing ourselves to fill up, and finally...
6. To express – verbally and nonverbally - this loving way of being through the way we respond and relate to others.

We recommend that you begin these practices in places and with people with whom you feel safe. You want everyone involved to have the intention to participate with simple open-minded curiosity and deep respect. There is a level of voluntary vulnerability in these practices that requires respectful collaboration and trustworthiness from the participants. (We call these practices, rather than exercises, because when they are done regularly, as with mindfulness, they cultivate a certain state of mind and gradually become skillful habits. Like learning a musical instrument, or a second language, as these habits develop with practice, they become a natural part of who we are and how we relate, whether we are thinking about them or not.)

Each of the stages mentioned above has several practices; in the following section we offer one key practice for each stage.

How to Open the Heart

Do not try to open your heart.

That would be a subtle movement of aggression toward your immediate embodied experience. Never tell a closed heart it must be more open; it will shut more tightly to protect itself, feeling your resistance and disapproval. A heart unfurls only when conditions are right; your demand for openness invites closure. This is the supreme intelligence of the heart.

Instead, bow to the heart in its current state. If it's closed, let it be closed; sanctify the closure. Make it safe; safe even to feel unsafe.

Trust that when the heart is ready, and not a moment before, it will open, like a flower in the warmth of the sun. There is no rush for the heart.

Trust the opening and the closing, too, the expansion and the contraction; this is the heart's way of breathing: safe, unsafe, safe, unsafe; *the beautiful fragility of being human, and all held in the most perfect love.*

~ Jeff Foster

THE PRACTICES

Mindfulness Practice

HERE'S A SIMPLE WAY TO PRACTICE CULTIVATING the foundational state of mind called "mindfulness."

The Practice:

Mindfulness practice can be done anywhere at any time, but it might be easiest to begin practicing on your own. Eventually it becomes even more powerful when practiced with others.

You can begin by getting into a comfortable sitting position. With your eyes open or closed, take a moment to simply listen to the sounds around you. Notice sounds that are constant and others that happen infrequently. Notice sounds that seem far away, and others that are closer. You might notice that some sounds evoke a reaction or an image or feeling. Is there any sound of breathing?

Just for a moment become aware of your breathing. Notice the flow of breath into and out of your body. There's no need to direct your breathing or to change it in any way. Simply notice it. Feel the sensation of breath in your nostrils, in the back of your throat. Feel the movement of your chest and ribcage as the breath moves in and out. Notice where you feel your body moving as you breathe.

Notice too, the quality of your noticing. Is it critical or analytical? Distracted or bored? Does it seem intense? Uncertain? Does your witnessing self have an attitude? Is it calm? Is it at ease?

Just notice any of this and then come back to simply following the flow of the breath as it moves into and out of your body.

Does the rhythm of your breathing seem to change as you observe it?

What other parts of your body do you become aware of as you pay attention to your breathing? Can you feel impulses or movements or what happens in your facial expression?

What else are you noticing? Are you aware of any sounds… thoughts… images… ?

What else is included in your present embodied and sensory experience? Just keep bringing your attention back to whatever shows up from moment to moment, within and around you.

Being With

"All real living is meeting."

~Martin Buber

WE ALL HAVE HABITS OF THOUGHT, MOOD and bodily organization that change when we are with another person. Our life experience has taught each of us that there is a certain way we need to be with others. These ways of being were modeled long ago by parents and other family members. We also learned it from the reactions of others to how we were being, and by getting messages from others about how we should be.

How we habitually relate with others comes partly out of our need to feel safe and our decisions and ideas about how to be safe. Some of it comes from a natural desire for approval, for a sense of belonging and acceptance... for love. We have all made decisions about who we think we are and who we need to be. Those decisions are now mostly outside of our awareness. They have become implicit.

Those unconscious ideas and assumptions about who we need to be, with and for others, have created a whole set of habits and patterns that are embodied; they inform our posture and our face, as well as our thinking and feelings when we are in relationship. We want to find out what those habits are so that we can put aside any that are unnecessary or that interfere with our being fully present when we are with another person. We want to introduce more relevant ones where necessary. The more conscious we become of our habit patterns, the more possibilities for choice and change become available to us.

Often just by noticing and recognizing our automatic reactions, we allow them to give way to a more spacious, calm, and ultimately compassionate way of being present. The first step is to simply become more aware of ourselves.

In this exercise, we want to study the differences in who we are being when the context changes from being alone to *being with* another person. We want to discover the habits governing this change because some of these habits make it difficult for us to shift into a state of Loving Presence. By becoming aware, we have more choice. We can begin to put aside whatever doesn't serve us.

T.S. Eliot, in his poem "The Love Song of J. Alfred Prufrock," says: *"prepare a face to meet the faces that you meet."*

How can we meet in a more loving way? If we can, why don't we? What are we doing instead?

The Practice of Being With:

This practice is done in pairs. Facing each other, begin with your eyes closed and take a few moments to get into a very quiet inward space; just let yourself begin to feel comfortable and open. To be open is to be sensitive and vulnerable. When you feel fairly comfortable and quiet inside, then open your eyes to look at your partner. Your partner's eyes might also be open or still closed. There will be some times when you both have your eyes open. You're each doing this at your own pace.

Just behold your partner; the intent here is mainly to observe yourself being with that person in front of you.

When you want to be back inside yourself, to get centered or simply to study what's happening, close your eyes again and be mindful of your present experience for a few moments.

What's going on inside your body and mind? If you notice any discomfort, what seems to have triggered it? What ideas might be involved?

After studying your experience this way for a few moments, get calm and centered and open your eyes again. For some of you this is easy. For those of you who are shy, this might be quite difficult at first, yet by the end you might find yourself sitting there very calmly with your eyes open and feeling connected in a sweet way with your partner. Whatever your experience is, after a few minutes, tell each other about it.

Groundlessness

MANY OF US HAVE A GREAT NEED TO KNOW, to assume we know or can know, to think we have the answers. This need to know creates a kind of noise when it comes to Loving Presence. As soon as we find ourselves in a place of knowing from our past experience, we might feel more secure in some way, but we are also very limited. This kind of knowing (assuming) creates a closed-in feeling. It limits our options and collapses possibilities. It's like going sailing with the boat firmly anchored. It makes it impossible to discover something new.

How do we find a place of not-knowing when we really do know a lot? Perhaps we could access a more open state of mind if we could drop our need to know, even for a moment. What then might be possible? How can we shift the focus away from the part of our mind that has some obvious answers (based on our memories and education and life experiences) and move toward another state of mind that really doesn't know for sure? This state might feel pretty groundless and even scary at first. Can we consider opening to the spaciousness it offers?

We do this Groundlessness practice to create this kind of spaciousness, to allow for the possibility of moments where we are more open to the sense of mystery.

In the practice of Loving Presence, Spacious Mind allows us to be with others differently and see them more clearly. Because we have no agenda but to simply be with them, we want to relax any intentions or preconceptions that would color our experience of them.

A spacious mind has flexible boundaries and allows for a greater capacity for quiet compassion. This quiet mind is not buzzing with concerns. Our internal voices are mostly still. Our body also relaxes. The noise is lowered, which helps greatly when we want to be aware of the subtleties of present time and company. A spacious mind is open to the element of surprise, to mystery, to learning and discovery. It doesn't need to rely on the habitual assumptions that our mind usually rests on when focused on certain tasks.

Spacious mind is different from ordinary consciousness in that it is not task-oriented. It's not motivated by survival, status, or the like. Typically, with any new sound or sight that we're aware of, there's an orientation period, a small amount of time where we stop whatever we're doing in order to judge the new situation. If we can identify the change as neither important nor dangerous, we simply go back to what we were doing before the interruption. Prey animals in the wild do this kind of orienting constantly. Watch a bird on the ground for a few moments. This orientation phase is about identifying. Once identification is over, the quality of attention changes, listening and looking all change (smelling, too!). The freshness of spaciousness is the freshness of the orientation phase, of remaining undecided, the "still-looking, not-sure-yet" phase.

As we do the Groundlessness practice to explore this kind of spaciousness, a whole new state of consciousness might suddenly come about. A shift might occur, a letting loose of the ties that bind us to ordinary experiences, to familiar selves. We might break away from all that is stale or distracting, like stepping from a crowded, noisy room into a peaceful garden filled with surprises that delight the senses and the soul.

The Practice of Groundlessness:

In this practice, one person asks another a series of very simple questions. The questions are about the other person and their life, the kind of questions you'd ask someone you've just met, or that you'd find on a questionnaire. All the questions are simple ones that any normal person would be able to answer easily, automatically, without hesitation.

In this practice, however, we want you to hesitate before answering.

Your job as the person hearing the questions is to watch the automatic answer that pops up in your mind and let it go by, and then search for a place inside where you really don't know the answer. If you find it, just hang out here for a little while and explore this space of not knowing; let yourself embrace not knowing and explore the feeling of it for a few moments. Then, finally, come back and say to your partner "I don't know." This lets your partner know that you are ready for another question. Don't be too quick to say, "I don't know." Take your time. Get curious about the embodied experience that goes with not knowing, not being so certain about ordinary things. (If there is no sincere way to answer, "I don't know" to a particular question after a few minutes of searching, just say, "Pass.")

Whether you've said, "I don't know," or "Pass," your partner comes up with another question and you repeat the process. Do this as many times as you like. Try going for about ten minutes, although you can decide to stop the exercise at any time when you're ready to discuss it. Then you can reverse roles and ask your partner the questions.

Here are a few typical questions and, to make it interesting for the questioners, you might try to intuitively come up with other questions for the particular person you're with.

How old are you?

Where is your home?

When were you born?

What is your name?

Who are your parents?

Where do you live?

What is your real work?

Who are you?

Seeing and Being Seen

BEFORE WE CAN TRULY BE WITH EACH OTHER, we need to discover and resolve some of our issues around seeing and being seen. Just being able to look at someone with the kind of innocence and fearlessness of an infant can be a gift to both the seer and the seen.

Much can be discerned about people by noticing the way they look, or don't look, at others. Do they avoid others' eyes? There might be strong cultural or personal differences here.

Many of us have learned to resist the experience of seeing deeply or of being seen. Family or cultural rules may have conditioned us to avoid looking at someone or seeing deeply, beyond what's on the surface. Our needs for safety and for approval may have resulted in habits of hiding behind a mask, presenting a façade or "cover story", or simply feeling a little uncomfortable about being seen by others.

Where fear is a habitual reaction to the prospect of intimacy, connecting visually is challenging. And yet, as poets and romantics know, "the eyes are the windows of the soul". Feelings can be read by looking into someone's eyes. Hostility and love, fear, anger, threat, grief, sadness, happiness and health—they're all written somehow in the eyes. In order for us to be in loving presence, to see beyond what's on the surface, we need to look receptively, calmly, openly and possibly for a long time into the other's eyes. We need to be able to fully take in the other, unafraid— to receive them completely. And for that, we need to be just as open about being looked at and okay about being seen.

To discover some of our issues about seeing and being seen, we want to commit ourselves to deep self-examination. The emotions and memories that this next practice can evoke usually come from deep parts of our very being, parts that control whatever states of mind we can enter as well as who we can be to be in relation to others. Of course, the state we're moving toward is Loving Presence. If we've somehow lost the knack of it—for example if we didn't have a loving caregiver when we were young—one way back to connection happens through this practice of seeing and being seen.

So, the essential idea and purpose of this practice is to discover and transform the issues or obstacles we have about seeing others and/or being seen. If we want to see deeply into others in order to be fully present for them just as they are, we need to study our own issues and attitudes about seeing and being seen. Here is a way to discover what gets in the way of seeing deeply into another person and/or letting ourselves be truly seen.

The Practice of Seeing and Being Seen:

In this practice, sit in pairs silently facing each other and attend to your inner experience while listening to some statements, either recorded or spoken by another person. The statements are offered slowly, one at a time, to allow you to notice what is evoked. Here are some of the statements:

*"It's okay to look at others
and see what's there."*

*"It's okay to really look at someone and
see them clearly..."*

*"It's okay to use your eyes as innocent children
use theirs, just being curious,
just simply looking..."*

*"It's safe to look at others and
actually see them..."*

"It's okay to be seen..."

"It's safe to let someone see you."

*"It's okay to let others look at you
and really see who you are."*

"There's no need for you to hide."

"It's safe to let someone see how you feel."

After hearing the statements, stay with your experience for a few moments; then talk with your partner about what happened. Report anything you noticed as you were hearing the statements. Talk about the actual experience and avoid going into interpretations and analyses about your reactions.

These next practices help to move us from this self-study phase into cultivating a more spacious mind. First we want to discover our habits and impulses; then we practice putting them on pause, relaxing what's automatic, and opening up some space for something new.

What follows is a practice for seeing in a new way...

Seeing Through

ONCE WE CAN ALLOW OURSELVES to see and be seen without embarrassment or fear, we're ready to "see through" to something deeply essential about others.

To see beyond the surface into the depths of someone, we want to see without thinking too much, without having too many ideas or preconceptions about the person we're seeing. Projections and prejudices interfere with this way of seeing.

Lao Tzu tells a story about a man who suspected his neighbor's son of stealing his axe. He couldn't help but see the little boy as a thief. But when the man's neighbor returned the axe he had borrowed, then he could see that the boy walked, looked, and spoke like any other child.

The idea that vision is only a passive sense reception is quite wrong. Scientist Rupert Sheldrake has done research on the feeling of being looked at. It demonstrates that people often know they are being looked at, even when they can't see who or what is looking at them. Seeing isn't a simple matter and neither is seeing through.

Being spacious and relaxed, we are able to receive very subtle signals, signals that we'd normally miss. From some deeper level within ourselves, we are able to perceive something essential about the person we're with. It might be something about their history, joys and disappointments, emotional pain, even a faint whisper of something sacred. There is a sweetness in almost every soul, much like the sweetness that emanates from infants.

This practice is about seeing deeply into others, finding something there that can awaken warm feelings in us.

One way to do this is to pay less attention to what the person is doing and more to how the person does things. We want to notice their posture, movements, gestures, tone of voice, verbal habits, their way of being, who they are—their style. There are, for instance, lots of ways to put down a book and each different way can reveal something. It might be careless or aggressive, precise or clumsy. It might reveal thoughtfulness, agitation, anger, fear, hurt, kindness, and so forth.

Everything someone does has stylistic qualities that can reveal something about them. If we take in several things at once and study the style of each, we can usually find a common element and this might suggest a particular characteristic quality or theme. This is a practice that can be done in a small willing group. It can be both scary and nourishing to be seen by others in this way.

In helping each other to feel safe enough to observe ourselves in this way, we need to be kind and friendly, interested, curious without judgment. And we need to keep ourselves open and spacious. Being spacious and without biased assumptions, we stay open to intuitive impressions and guesses. Impressions that might be insightful show up easily. We don't need to have any solid reasons for our impressions about each other as we remind ourselves that they might be just guesses. We want to be like artists and poets, playful and creative, letting our imagination assist us to see more than what seems obvious.

The Practice of Seeing Through:

One person does several things in a sequence while one or more partners simply witness.

The first thing the person does is simply stand or sit before the partners. The partners do what is called a blink: they open their eyes just for a second to take in an impression of the person.

The person then says a few lines of a childhood verse like "Mary Had a Little Lamb" or something comparable while the partners just listen (eyes open or closed).

Next, the person gets up and walks a few steps away, picks something up or pretends to, and walks back to the partners while they simply watch.

Lastly, the person says something personally meaningful, saying it first with their eyes open and then saying the same statement with their eyes closed while the partners observe.

Partners: Ask yourselves, is there an essential pattern here? What seems characteristic about the person's style? (Like moving fast or tentatively, speaking and moving softly, performing everything confidently or seeming shy, and so on...)

Of course this kind of witnessing can be practiced any time without speaking about it to the person being observed. We want to remind ourselves of the difference and distinction between our observations and impressions on the one hand and our guesses or interpretations on the other. We want to become sincerely fascinated by observing others, to let our imagination play in a space outside of any judgmental attitudes.

As we learn ways to see more deeply into people, we create the possibility of seeing those aspects of others which will most inspire and nourish us. We want to be able to see and appreciate the essential beauty of people, and to let ourselves feel good about that. We want to begin to open up to a kind of spiritual and non ego-centered nourishment.

What follows next is a way to begin to set the mood for Loving Presence and the taking in of this kind of spiritual nourishment. We call it *Priming the Pump.*

Priming the Pump

IN THIS PRACTICE WE SIT WITH OTHERS to verbally exchange memories and stories about people that have made a big positive difference for us, people who have been a blessing in our lives. Simply remembering and talking about the qualities of such people and the gifts they have brought to our lives can prepare us to see these same qualities in others. Mainly we do this sharing to generate a feeling shift in the group, an energy that is palpable.

So, like kids around a campfire, we tell each other stories. The mood created here leads quickly to a sense of being nourished just by being with others, the kind of nourishment that will sustain Loving Presence. The state of mind of Loving Presence begins with feeling a friendly interest and an appreciation of others, especially appreciating their special gifts and good qualities.

The Practice of Priming the Pump:

In a small group, each person takes a few minutes to talk about a special person who has touched your life in a nourishing and inspirational way, a person that has been a gift to you. The others simply listen silently, without commenting or asking questions, just listening and taking you in.

After everyone has shared, discuss the effect of this kind of sharing for a few minutes. What kind of feelings and mood did this sharing generate in you, both as talker and as listener? How did it seem to change your state of mind and your relationship to each other?

The Priming the Pump practice leads naturally to the next stage in this practice of Loving Presence, the nourishment stage. Here's something you can do by yourself or in pairs or a small group..

"Nothing else matters half so much,
To reassure one another,
To answer each other.
Everyone has inside himself,
- what shall I call it?
A piece of good news."

- Ugo Betti

Search for Inspiration

EACH PERSON IS A SOURCE OF "GOOD NEWS" ... of a kind of spiritual nourishment that we can find if we see deeply into them and suspend any agenda other than searching for, finding, and taking in this nourishment.

This kind of nourishment has nothing to do with our ego; it is "soul food" in the same way as great music or a sweet friendship. We could also call it inspiration.

If we want to be loving, we have to feel the pleasure of inspiration, the pleasure of our spirits being lifted and filled. Our purpose is to find this pleasure by seeing deeply into the person we're with. If we can do that, we will respond spontaneously with a loving feeling. We'll feel more compassionate, and naturally want to offer them our time, our attention, our presence and our care. For this to happen, we deliberately search for and find sources of goodness and inspiration in the other. That's the point of this practice.

There's some essential goodness in everyone. According to a Buddhist premise, the ground of being is unconditioned good. We want to see behind the level of someone's behaviors, or their problems and symptoms. We want to look for what's good, what's right, what's inspiring.

Here are some sources of this kind of nourishment that we've found: beauty, innocence, gentleness, sweetness, vulnerability, a person's humanity—ordinary, dirt-common humanity. We have seen how courageous some people are, how loyal, how loving. We have also seen the depth of their pain and how they have nevertheless endured, with determination, perseverance, even stubbornness.

We sometimes see something universal and mythic, even heroic. This once happened for me [Ron] when a client was talking about the baby daughter about to be born to him and his wife. He was about to become a father. As a father himself, I knew what was coming for him. I could see that he was making a transition that fathers have been making for millions of years. All the genetic and cultural wisdom embedded in our species seemed to be converging in this particular father-to-be. I saw him, not just as the individual he was, but also that he carried within him this thing called fatherhood. He represented for me, at that moment, all the men who ever were fathers. I could talk to him about how that would unfold for him and that he wasn't facing this coming of his daughter completely unprepared. Time and chance for endless eons had been his preparation. A billion fathers had paved the way. He had within him, if he could hearken to it, the wisdom of fatherhood, and this would serve him well in his new adventure."

This same kind of information is part of the myths of all the peoples of the world. The same wisdom allows us to see others as mythic or archetypal beings. It is the doctor as healer, the warrior in those who protect others, the mother archetype in people who feed us and listen to us. These identities shape decisions and events for each of us. In opening to nourishment like this in others, we might find it in the spirit of these universals.

Nourishment can also be found in the more specifically personal. Perhaps we'll see the child in an adult person. Perhaps tenderness or vulnerability. We've seen both necessary pain and unnecessary suffering. Both can evoke feelings of compassion.

So, we look for these kinds of things: for grace and beauty and essential goodness, for the mythic and universal, for a depth of feeling or vulnerability. We even see stubbornness or a fierce survival instinct and find these inspiring. It doesn't have to be a conventionally positive aspect to be something we can appreciate.

And there's always something. One person is deeply h
Another has great courage. Another is talented, or humorous, or
poetic. Something is available in every moment.

The Practice of Search for Inspiration:

In pairs or in a small group, one person at a time talks about
something significant or meaningful in their life. It's an opportunity
to be witnessed and listened to in a very spacious, loving way.

Your primary job as listener is to stay open to those aspects of
the situation and of the person talking that will give you spiritual
nourishment. Its not so much about following the narrative. It's more
about how beautiful the storyteller looks or sounds or how wonderful
it is to be with someone in such a safely intimate situation.

It might start with the simple enjoyment of your curiosity and
discovery. It might be about seeing vulnerability or humanity or
even signs of present or past suffering in the other. It might be their
strength, courage, honesty, or their vulnerability.

Search for something universal, or archetypal, for grace or beauty,
for something essentially good that you can see in this person. Find
a way to let that quality fill you up; open your heart and take it in.
Listen to the person in silence without verbally responding, without
making any comments or interventions. Just let yourself be inspired
and nourished somehow by the person who is talking.

Do this for as long as it feels right to the person talking, and
then discuss it together. Don't refer to the content of the story.
Simply talk about your own experience. What was it like to listen
in this way? To be listened to this way? What were the sources of
nourishment you found? Let everyone have a turn to be the talker.

The state of mind we are calling Loving Presence begins to
emerge spontaneously as a result of the sequence of practices we have
presented. It emerges naturally in certain life situations anyway, and
these practices are simply about cultivating this state more predictably
and easily, in any human interaction. Next we offer a way to prepare
yourself for this state of mind, whether on your own or with others...

Loving Presence

Loving Presence, first, for yourself!

Begin by taking time to relax and quiet the mind. Bringing your mind and body into a calm and relaxed state is the first step. A regular mindfulness practice makes it easier to call for this shift when you need it. Find a practice that works for you to quiet your mind and relax your body, perhaps using breath or meditation or yoga or using a guided relaxation CD or music. You might have already discovered that a simple mindfulness practice is one of the most effective ways of bringing yourself into a quieter state.

Bring to mind someone who is one of the most loving people you know. As you think about this person, notice what happens to you. Does your breathing change? How does your body feel when you think about this person? Just be with your embodied experience for a few minutes.

Now think about someone you love or have loved. Stay for a few moments simply paying attention to your physical sensations and the embodied experience of feeling loving, even as a memory. Ask yourself, what unnecessary and irrelevant habits sometimes interfere with these peaceful and loving feelings and keep you from being fully present in a loving way?

Take a moment to think about someone you care about, someone you feel compassionate toward. Think about them enough to actually generate some feelings of appreciation and love and let these feelings begin to stabilize. Notice the source of these feelings in your body. Go back and forth from thinking about the person to noticing the feelings you are having. It is as if you are getting in touch with the part of you that is capable of more compassion and love. It is said that gratitude is the key to opening the heart. How does your heart seem to open with these thoughts? Stay with these feelings and let them stabilize before the next step. Now replace the original person in your mind's eye with another person, also someone easy for you to feel positive toward, and then with another.

At some point, once you have cultivated the Loving Presence state of mind thinking about others, bring in an awareness of yourself—perhaps even a part of yourself you may feel critical about. It might help to imagine this part of yourself as a little child and notice something about her needs and feelings. Can you let this image call up from you the same feelings of love and kindness that you can generate easily for others? When you are able to do this, notice whether or not this child part seems to realize that you feel kinder, less critical, perhaps more loving toward her.

When we can notice and interrupt old habits of self-criticism or self-abandonment, we begin to change the quality of our relationship both to ourself and to others. Our inner and outer relationships transform into a healthier and more loving expression of our essential self, of the spirit of who we truly are.

> *"Be what you are: intelligence*
> *and love in action."*
> - Nisargadatta Maharaj

The basic idea of this whole practice is that it is possible to set up a specific pattern of interaction between two or more people that makes a healthy emotional connection possible. The creation of that specific pattern is what this practice of Loving Presence, is about. It is relevant to the interaction between any two or more sentient beings.

Loving Presence with other people:

When emotional healing happens, it happens in a certain context—the right place, the right time and, especially, the right people in the right state of mind. The context helps initiate the healing process and sustains it as it unfolds. When anyone remains attentive and loving, with no other agenda than to see deeply and to take inspiration from what is seen, a context for healing and change has been created.

If you are a therapist, your clients will recognize that help and healing is possible, that a loving, attentive person is present and available. That alone is often enough to evoke a spontaneous experience of emotional healing. Something in the client recognizes the situation as an opportunity to bring forth their deepest feelings and a chance to unburden them. Painful memories and feelings need this kind of companionship for healing. When emotional healing happens, it starts spontaneously, easily, and almost immediately with someone being in a loving presence state of mind. After the readiness of the client, the most significant influence on any therapeutic process is the state of mind of the therapist. Loving presence.

But you don't need to be a therapist to offer this kind of healing presence for another. We are all capable of it.

> *"I learned how to listen,*
> *to listen with a still heart,*
> *with a waiting, open soul,*
> *without passion, without desire,*
> *without judgments,*
> *without opinions. "*
> ~ Herman Hesse

Loving Presence in Pairs (or a small group):

One person talks about an emotionally powerful event in his or her life. The listener is following the story but mostly staying in touch with all the sources of nourishment and inspiration available in each moment of listening. Whatever sources you find, be sure to take them in and let them nourish and inspire you as you listen. Listen without speaking or making any interventions. Don't ask questions or make any comments. Simply be in Loving Presence. Open your heart, pay close attention, relax and listen with open-hearted warmth and without judgment. You have nothing else to do (with the exception of the instructions below). No responsibilities beyond your own experience of being inspired and taking in nourishment.

> **Talker:** please remember to look at your listener, at least part of the time. Notice how it feels to be with this person who is simply witnessing you in Loving Presence.

> **Listener:** if the person telling the story isn't looking at you, gently remind them, perhaps just with a gentle touch. Study your impulses to do or say things and just come back to your search for inspiration to be in loving presence.

Continue as long as it seems right for both, especially the talker. Then discuss your experiences (not the issue or story the person was talking about). Just talk about the experience of Loving Presence and how it affected you.

"A Loving Present":

Loving Presence is relevant to being with others in all kinds of interpersonal situations. Here's a personal story about this practice. One young mother we know decided to take the practice of Loving Presence home to her two little daughters. She offered them each a few minutes of Loving Presence at their bedtime. She explained that they could tell her anything and she would not ask questions or give advice…she would simply listen and appreciate and love them while they spoke about whatever. They could also simply be with her in silence if they wished. The daughters came to treasure this time together with their mother. In fact, after a couple of weeks, they told their mother, "We want Daddy to give us a loving present at bedtime too!"

The final stage of the practice of Loving Presence involves responding to each other. Loving responses are possible and more likely when we have practiced cultivating the state of Loving Presence. A few simple steps will strongly influence the way we respond from this state.

Here's a way to practice this with a partner or group...

Before You Speak

THIS IS A FOUR-STEP PROCESS, steps which become skillful habits after a while. First, we want to make our responses relevant to present experience. This is essential. It means we have to actively and continuously pay attention to the other person's expression of what's happening for them in present time. The tendency for many of us is to fall into normal conversation. But the conversational thoughts and ideas that arise for us might have nothing to do with what is actually being felt by the person in the moment.

The first step in this practice is to bring ourselves into present time. We want to notice something going on right now, possibly for us but especially for the other person. Maybe it's some excitement or worry about something. It might be a sense of sadness or concern or simply an expressive gesture or tone of voice. These are the things we want to notice.

The second step is to name what we've noticed for ourselves, at first describing it in silence, only for ourselves. This is like a novelist's task, one that writers face all the time – putting feelings, images and vague ideas into words. What makes this somewhat challenging is that we are listening to someone speak, while at the same time we are trying to formulate in our own words something that is quite possibly unrelated to what the person is talking about.

Our usual habit, when someone is speaking, is to focus primarily on the words, taking in the ideas, implications and images coming to us. Often, that requires real concentration. This happens for therapists, but also for friends, teachers, parents, spouses. Here, whatever our role, we want to concentrate on something entirely different. We want to try putting into our own words something we've noticed about the person while the person is talking to us. This takes practice.

What we're naming is something that's happening, but isn't necessarily being talked about. The person might have feelings or an attitude about what they're talking about, but not mention them; they might not even be aware of them. These things are definitely part of the communication, only they're nonverbal. They're in the background. They are expressed through the tone of voice, pacing, emphasis, posture, movements, gestures and facial expressions. We often respond to these nonverbal elements of communication without thinking about them or naming them. This time, we're deliberately but silently naming them to ourselves.

We also want to empathize before we speak. We want our responses to be loving ones. This is the third step: being nourished. We want to appreciate something we've noticed about the other person. If we are already in a Loving Presence state of mind, having searched for and found inspiration, this appreciation is already present.

So, before we speak, we let ourselves appreciate something we've noticed.

All this happens before we offer any verbal response, which is the last step. With this preparation, we need only allow our spontaneous thoughts and feelings to generate our response. We don't need to be cautious or very deliberate about this. This process is not determined by cognitive thinking; it is influenced and guided by the kind of feelings which have been deliberately brought forth through steps one, two and three. Whatever we say at this point from this kind of empathic connection will be in tune with the other. It's more likely to be relevant and appropriate, without being calculating. It will be loving and nurturing without our making any effort to make it so.

This is Loving Presence in action and it totally depends on what we have been doing before we open our mouths to speak.

The Practice of Before You Speak:

To practice Loving Presence as part of a normal two-person interaction, spend fifteen minutes or so working in the following way:

In pairs, one person talks. The listener practices Loving Presence. Listener, before any response, wait for the talker's signal that it is your turn, and before you say anything, do these three things first:

- **Notice** something in present time about the person who's talking; something about what kind of human situation this is that is happening now, right in front of you. All of this is different from the more limited activity of following the story and thinking about the content of what the person is telling you.

- **Name** what you have noticed, for yourself. Not out loud, but silently as part of your thinking and intuition. Put what you are noticing into words, for yourself.

- This thing you've named for yourself, **appreciate it**! Take it in! Feel it! Digest it! Feel the gift of noticing it. Let yourself be touched or inspired by it. Savor the quality of it as food for the soul. Let your whole being participate in taking in this inspiration and nourishment. Finally...

- **Respond** from this place of appreciation; allow something you say or do next simply to arise from your heart and come easily to mind. Relax and see what natural responses occur to you spontaneously when you are resting in this attitude of gratitude and appreciation. Trust that an appropriate, loving impulse will emerge without undue effort. If no verbal response arises naturally, simply continue to listen in loving presence and allow your experience of feeling nourished and inspired to soften your face and shine from your demeanor. We call it "beaming". Don't fake it. Let it happen naturally.

Continue listening and responding in this way for as long as ten or fifteen minutes. Afterward, discuss your experiences together —both as the listener and the talker, as well as any observers or witnesses present.

These are the basic steps and key practices for each step but there are many additional and complementary practices that will enhance and enrich your capacity for this amazing state of mind.

WHERE LOVING PRESENCE IS NEEDED

*From our very first breath, we are in relationship.
With that indrawn draft of air, we become joined to
everything that ever was, is and ever will be.
When we exhale, we forge that relationship
by virtue of the act of living.*

*Our breath commingles with all breath, and we are
a part of everything. That's the simple fact of things.
We are born into a state of relationship, and our ceremonies
and rituals are guides to lead us deeper into
that relationship with all things. Big lesson?
Relationships never end; they just change.*

*In believing that lies the freedom to carry compassion,
empathy, love, kindness and respect into and through
whatever changes. We are made more by that practice.*

~ Richard Wagamese

Where is loving presence needed most?

THE PRACTICE OF LOVING PRESENCE HAS widespread applications in both personal and professional life situations. It provides the best context for any kind of healing relationship. Wherever you feel most helpless may be the very place calling you to be in Loving Presence. Whoever you find it hardest to be with may be the one who is inviting you to interrupt your habitual ways and move into a more spacious state of mind. Whenever you feel your heart in pain, it may be a signal that your capacity for love is ready to expand into new dimensions. Loving Presence is a useful way of being:

- With your partner
- With children
- With friends
- With family
- With the sick or dying
- With patients/clients
- With a group
- With yourself

The way of healing is not mechanical, not linear or logical. A cut finger needs no theories. It knows the way, and, if the path is made easy, it will heal. What makes the path to healing emotional hurts possible is the love and attention of a strong, calm, and responsive presence. Some work still has to be done, but it is so much easier in the presence of a loving being. This is what so many of us love about our pet dogs. They see only the best in us and they love us unconditionally, just as we are.

This way of being present is our natural birthright, but many of us have forgotten it, or got out of the habit. Appreciating our fellow human beings is a natural human capacity, present to some degree in every child born. Unless it has been damaged or destroyed by terrible circumstances, it is there in everyone we meet. We can find in ourselves and we can find it in each other. We can offer it to those we serve, whether as friends or therapists. If we are not taught how to love and be present this way, we're living with weights on our hearts and minds, and blinders on our eyes and ears. We're missing some of the most nourishing and fulfilling experiences that life has to offer.

Here follow some ideas for using the practice of Loving Presence with friends, family, or at work.

With your Life Partner

The stars come up spinning every night,
bewildered in love.
They'd grow tired with that revolving,
if they weren't. They'd say,
"How long do we have to do this!"

~ Rumi

IN A COMMITTED RELATIONSHIP SUCH AS A MARRIAGE, the practice of Loving Presence enhances the level of trust, appreciation, communication and intimacy you can have with your life partner.

Sometimes it is the people closest to us, people we love the most, that we have the hardest time appreciating. Many of the Loving Presence practices can be done at home as a way of shifting a difficult situation, transforming how we perceive each other, and how we're reacting. It's possible to start by choosing to focus on something to appreciate about our partner every day. This can be challenging if our habit is to build a list of the things that annoy us. It's something one person can do without even talking about it. But it's immensely more powerful to do it together.

Perhaps you and your partner will decide to set aside regular times to do one or more of the Loving Presence practices together. Even sitting together and practicing mindfulness for a few minutes regularly in silent togetherness can be a powerful way to create a kind of "limbic resonance" and deeper connection with each other.

We suggest you start with *Mindfulness* and then with *Being With,* simply looking at one another for a few minutes in mindfulness, without talking, each of you witnessing your own internal experience. This practice alone can be a powerful contribution to greater intimacy and love.

A follow-up practice is *Being With 1-2-3.* Part One is simply looking at each other and noticing your internal reactions and impulses without saying or doing anything. Part Two is to intentionally look for signs of suffering in your partner—let yourself see or imagine their challenges and their pain. Then notice what is called up inside you. Finally, in Part Three, search for something positive in your partner. See something that touches or nourishes you, that inspires you. Again, be with your own experience. What happens differently within you with each way of seeing, of being with?

Other practices to use with your mate as a way of exploring this approach include one called *Intimacy,* where you simply have a dialogue while maintaining eye contact, but you only speak in one or two statements at a time about your own present moment experience, and you don't interrupt each other.

Or as you listen to your partner talk to you, practice the *Search for Inspiration and Nourishment.* After your partner has finished saying whatever they want to say, pause for a moment and then simply report how you were nourished. Pause after this before discussing. Take turns being the talker and the listener.

Some couples make a commitment to an intentional practice of loving presence and choose to spend up to half an hour regularly doing one or more of the practices and then talking about their experience. It can be life changing.

With Children

"Our attachment relationships affect how we see others and how we see ourselves."
~ Daniel Siegel and Mary Hartzell

DURING THE VIET NAM WAR, I [Ron] went to hear some speeches in San Francisco's beautiful Grace Cathedral, a very large, impressive church. It was the right setting for what was taking place there: protest against the war. Though I'm not particularly religious, I felt awe-inspired by both the setting and the topic. The people who spoke included the head of the church, Norman Vincent Peale, and two others who were Nobel prize winners. One was a physicist. The other, neurophysiologist George Wald, argued eloquently, "We can ask a very simple question about this war: Is it good for children?" The answer was obvious. War is not good for children. He went on to name other things, like atomic weapons, air pollution, the destruction of the environment and of each he asked, "Is it good for children?" To me it seems a very sensible criterion, that clear and simple question: Is it good for children?

When I remember that speech, I ask myself, "What is good for children?" Here's my answer. I've been reading a book called, The Developing Mind, by Daniel J. Siegal. The chapter that came to mind is about attachment. It's about patterns of emotional connections that children develop as a result of the kind of parenting they receive. These attachment patterns are the primary determiners of the kind of personalities and relationships the child will grow up to have. They shape the child's whole life.

One of the things Siegel states is this: if a parent has unresolved trauma or grief, it will negatively effect the children. In other words, it's not good for children. Unresolved trauma or grief creates pain and suffering, not only in these distressed individuals, but for their children as well. Siegel says, "... lack of resolution can permit dysfunction to continue across the generations." These children have a marked inability to regulate emotional responses and the flow of states of mind.

It's important to remember that this results from **unresolved** trauma or grief. If these things are resolved, they don't affect the children.

When the parent's issues are unresolved and the parent cannot regulate his or her emotional responses, the parent is unpredictable for the child. The parent has unpredictable mood swings and the child cannot find a secure way to be with that parent. Because the child is so dependent, its primary need is for a parent it can depend upon. If the parent is unreliable, the child cannot create a reliable world for itself. The child forms what is called a disorganized/ disoriented attachment pattern. This is a disturbance of a basic kind, a painful deficiency in the development of the self, a defect in the ability to control (regulate) emotions that places gross limitations on all relationships. If and when the disturbed child later becomes a parent, the unresolved disturbance gets passed to his or her children.

So, when we ask, "what is good for children?" the answer is clear. What's good for children is that their caregivers are reliable in this way: the caregivers can form a relationship with the child in which the child's needs are consistently recognized and met. Among these needs is the need to live in a world that fits together and makes sense. If the parents' world fits together and makes sense, that helps the child to create a world for itself that fits together and makes sense. That's not all though. The child needs to learn to regulate his or her emotions. Consistent affect regulation on the part of the caregiver makes that possible. So, we know it is good for children if the parents are reliably calm, reliably available, reliably sensitive to the child's needs, and reliable providers.

In therapy, when trauma and grief issues need to be resolved, the therapist must have exactly these same qualities: calm, presence, sensitivity, availability, and the skills to help the client create a world that fits together and makes sense, a world where we can find safety, comfort and meaning. These are basic to psychological health and therefore, to good caregiving. And, it needs to be said: psychotherapy is caregiving. One or all of these basic experiences—safety, comfort, meaning—are missing for disturbed people. Providing these things for them is how the chain of grief, trauma and unfulfilled lives can be broken.

Something of this availability and kindness can be present not just in therapy and not just between children and their parents, but in all our daily interactions. In all our relationships, where we are reliably calm, sensitive and available, we help create a better world, not only for our children (who especially need that), but for everybody. Kindness and availability—its good for you, good for me and it's good for children.

It can be very easy to practice Loving Presence with children. Appreciating their curiosity about the world, their determination to learn (and get their needs met), their amazement at the world— these are things that are easy to find joy in. Of course all these things can be very inconvenient for adults, but slowing down enough to connect with that curiosity, that determination, that amazement, is what it's all about.

Often when a child is upset, parents also become upset. They might feel embarrassed because they think other parents nearby are judging them, they might be in a hurry that day, they might have unresolved trauma from their own childhood about what happens when a child gets upset. Often this results in parents or caregivers telling the child to stop being upset. When this doesn't work they offer a "consequence," so children will be motivated to stop expressing their feelings. This may gain compliance in the short term, but what the child learns in the long term is that feelings are not to be expressed, and that the people they rely on are not available to help them with feelings that are too big, or with needs they don't have words to express.

Children often do not have the tools to work through what they are experiencing or feeling. They need help. If parents are able to broaden their perspective of the child enough to see how their current behavior actually makes sense, they are more likely to know what the child really needs in that moment.

Teachers also have a unique opportunity to benefit themselves and their students by bringing Loving Presence to the classroom. This state of mind can be an antidote to burnout because the practice fills us up. When teachers practice Loving Presence it creates an atmosphere that helps children learn. Choosing to focus on appreciating something about the children in the room allows teachers to feel warmth and respect, and creates a healthy learning environment for teachers and students. When children feel appreciated, they are more likely to relax their defenses and experience a sense of belonging and connectedness. This is essential for positive learning outcomes.

In Daniel Goleman's bestselling book, *Emotional Intelligence,* he focuses on the importance - for children and adults alike - of emotional intelligence or "social and emotional learning" (SEL) Many U.S. schools now teach SEL to both teachers and students. From Goleman's website: *"Helping children improve their self-awareness and confidence, manage their disturbing emotions and impulses, and increase their empathy pays off not just in improved behavior but in measurable academic achievement."*

A mindfulness practice is very good for children and can be

an important part of their social emotional learning. Mindfulness helps children learn to notice their own feelings and to be aware of the feelings of others. Teaching mindfulness in a classroom doesn't have to be a big deal, and it doesn't have to take much time. The key is to teach children to be quietly and mindfully aware of themselves, even for just a few moments—to just simply notice something about their present moment experience without needing it to be anything in particular. The important thing is to build an atmosphere of acceptance and respect so students feel safe.

Teachers can find many ways of supporting children to relate to each other with respect and appreciation. Stories are a wonderful way to introduce such concepts and to create and discuss experiences of how to see others and how to respond. Stories that talk about the kinds of challenges where someone finds alternatives to becoming angry, resentful, or revengeful, can be used to explore different ways of dealing with such situations.

Following a story with some personal sharing, drawing, creative movement, or a Loving Presence practice such as this one, called *"Who do you see?"*, can turn a simple storytelling experience into an important lesson about emotional intelligence.

Who Do You See?

In this exercise, the teacher asks the children to close their eyes after first taking a slow look around the classroom at each other. The first step can be a simple demonstration of how much or little we remember based on what we've noticed. Ask questions like: "Who is wearing a blue shirt? Which person who usually wears glasses is not wearing them right now?" The children try to answer the questions without opening their eyes. Next, tell the children that you are going to suggest something for them to imagine, and then they are to open their eyes, look around, and notice what is different about what they see.

A simple suggestion to give them is to imagine that a story

they've read will be made into a movie and that everyone in the class is an actor trying out for a part in the film. Or have the children imagine that they see each other as the kind of people that were in the story. If the story talked about certain qualities, (like courage), have the children imagine that each child in the room has done something brave or heroic.

Have the children spend a minute or so imagining each one of these ideas before they open their eyes to look at each other, and then to close their eyes again for a moment before sharing with each other what they saw.

This exercise is great for people of all ages. It demonstrates how we filter out certain things and see mostly what we expect to see in each other. When people have known each other for a long time, they tend to limit their seeing to what is predictable and known. Zen meditators practice seeing with "beginner's mind" in order to open up more space in their awareness to allow in more of life's wonder and magic.

Blink Exercises

Blink exercises are also fun for children and adults alike. Young children still have access to much of the sensitivity and intuition that might get lost later on as the more logical and rational aspects of mind are emphasized.

One version of the Blink exercise that helps children to retain some of their magical and wonder-filled ways of seeing is to have them stand in two lines facing each other. The children in one line close their eyes. Their partners then change places and stand in front of someone else who has their eyes closed.

At first, little kids will peek. That's okay. They'll learn that it can be fun to keep their eyes closed and that there are no mistakes. You aren't asking them to guess who is in front of them now, though they might. You could, for example, invite them to imagine a color for the person in front of them, and then to open their eyes just for a second or two (a blink) and notice what color they see.

Some will see the color of their partner's shirt. Some might see a color that is more symbolic, perhaps describing the other child's emotional state. There is no wrong answer. Then they move around and do it with a few others. After a few turns, the blinkers become the blinkees and vice versa.

Another version is to just let the blinkers get an impression of the other child as a character in a story they've just heard or read, or they make up a story about the impression they got—perhaps about a mythical character—or perhaps the main character in a familiar book at a certain point in the story.

It's important to teach children and adults alike that our impressions usually say more about us than about the other person. It's up to the other person to say if someone's impression has anything to do with them. Even young children can learn about projections this way.

There are lots of variations of the Blink exercise. One is to suggest to the blinkers that when they open their eyes, they'll see someone who's just come to their front door. "Who is it and what are they doing at your door?" Or they open their eyes just for a second and get a glimpse of someone who's standing in the schoolyard... "What are they doing? How are they feeling?" (This is an excellent way to teach more about empathy.)

If you have told or read a story about a gift (ie. "Gift of the Magi"), an exercise to use with students is a variation of the Walking Toward exercise.

Walking Toward

In this practice, done in groups of three, one person (A) stands a few feet away from the other two (B and C). B closes her eyes. C is a watcher or witness. B takes a moment just to notice herself and anything she's feeling or sensing. She shares this with C, her witness. Then she opens her eyes and looks at A. This is a signal for A to very slowly walk toward B. Something will start to happen for B and she can close her eyes to pay attention to it. This means A stops approaching.

When B is ready to continue, she opens her eyes again and A starts to walk toward her again very slowly. Now C leans toward B and whispers "What's the gift?" B closes her eyes again and A stops walking. When B opens her eyes this time she is looking for or imagining a gift that A has.

For young children, this can mean any imaginary present. For older children or adults, this can refer to something about the person (A) that can be appreciated as a gift… their honesty, for example, or their friendship, their gentleness, sense of humor, et cetera.

This exercise can provide an opportunity to teach children that everything about us has another side: that another person's apparent aloofness, for example, can be perceived as strength or independence; or that someone's unpredictability can also be appreciated as spontaneity.

Some of the exercises that teachers themselves can use, in professional groups or individually, to develop this way of listening and witnessing, include Groundlessness and Looking for Inspiration and Nourishment.

The ability to remember to be nourished, even inspired, by anyone, at any time, is invaluable for a teacher who wants to stay energized, avoid burnout, and both practice and model loving presence in the classroom.

With Friends

*Love is the only force capable of transforming
an enemy into a friend.*
~ Martin Luther King

FROM EARLY CHILDHOOD, WE ARE CONCERNED with acceptance, acknowledgment, and appreciation because in our earliest years, for much longer than most species, we need to be taken care of by others. If our lives depend on someone else, it is essential that they want to care for us. We need to be loved—our survival depends on it. Developing our independence (as well as healthy interdependence) is a gradual and natural shift away from being taken care of primarily by others to taking care of ourselves and others. Along the way we struggle with the seeming paradox of relationship and freedom, of being loved without being dependent, of separateness and belonging, of a need for privacy and a need for connection. Finding a healthy balance of interdependence can take a lifetime.

Whether we make friends easily or not, having friends is important for all of us. We humans, to a greater or lesser degree, are social creatures. We may make friends where we work, or find them in a social group. For many people friendships become their chosen family. And, like family relationships, friendships can be relationships in which we grow into ourselves and toward each other, or filled with misunderstanding, reactions, perceived slights or insults. Our friendships can be strengthened by sharing the practice of Loving Presence.

The practice of Loving Presence asks us to choose, over and over, to focus our attention on what we appreciate and enjoy and admire about our friends. Of course there may still be some things about them we don't like and need to talk about in a respectful way, but there's little ground for satisfying communication without Loving Presence.

The doorway to health and healing, to remembering our wholeness, is found in recovering our true belongingness. Through finding ourselves to be part of a greater whole, we can rediscover the truth of our own wholeness. Through loving others and letting others love us, we are weaving together a tapestry of peaceful human relationships and community. Any or all of the practices described in this book can be used to deepen the friendships you have.

Perhaps you and one or more friends would like to create a Loving Presence practice group to meet regularly and spend an hour or more doing one or two of the practices together before whatever else you do. Take turns deciding which practices to use, starting with simple mindfulness, and remember to spend part of the time noticing and sharing about how it's changing your friendship.

With Family

The bond that links your true family is not one of blood, but of respect and joy in each others' lives.

~ Richard Bach

IF YOU WANT TO IMPROVE YOUR ONGOING RELATIONSHIPS with family members generally, and especially with aging parents, the practice of Loving Presence is a great place to begin. You might realize that your relatives, especially your parents, can be the most challenging and difficult people for you to be with in this loving and nonjudgmental way. Practicing Loving Presence with total strangers can often be easier than with family! On the other hand, whatever amount of Loving Presence you can practice and experience with your family will be transformative.

As parents and older family members age, and the balance of care tips, it can be confusing and upsetting for everyone. Parents may begin to lose the ability to manage their lives in a healthy way (if they were ever able to do so), and it can be very difficult to figure out the best way to help them without losing track of your own needs. Any unresolved issues or patterns of behavior can become more challenging as the family comes together (or doesn't) under pressure. The practice of Loving Presence can refocus you long enough to see parents anew, and to respond rather than react.

To change the ways you relate to a parent or other close family members, use the practice of Loving Presence, making a choice to focus on anything about them that you can appreciate; see them as they are in each moment and not as you have come to expect them to be.

Loving Presence gives us another way of relating. Like any new habit it can be challenging at first, but if we choose to see through the surface image we have of someone and perceive, perhaps for the first time, the spirit and essence of who they really are, this evokes a new appreciation and understanding that becomes almost effortless, not because we're trying to be generous, but as a natural response.

For example, practice the search for inspiration and nourishment whenever you are with your parents or other family members. With some family members this practice will come more naturally, and with others it is truly a challenge. But it is a challenge worth taking and the rewards will be felt by everyone.

A person who intuits the ways of the heart
has a better chance of living well.
~ from <u>A General Theory of Love</u>

With the Sick or Dying

WHEN WE HAVE THE PRIVILEGE OF KNOWING SOMEONE who is very ill or dying, we are being presented with an opportunity to step past our own goals and issues and feelings and simply meet the other person where they are. It's enough to just be there. Of course it can be frightening and painful and frustrating when there is little or nothing that can be done to help them. The real gift we can give someone who is very ill or dying is our time, and a willingness to be present with them. Finding something inspiring or touching in a person's struggle with illness or death can serve as an antidote to the fear we might have that there is nothing we can do to help. It seems counterintuitive, but searching for the beauty in people, no matter how ill they are, allows us to be radically present.

When someone, especially someone you care about, is ill or distressed, or overcome emotionally, it can trigger strong reactions. If you can, stay calm; if that is too hard, be kind to yourself about that. Along with staying calm, it's important to keep your attention focused on the present moment. Your mind may be caught up in other things, like worrying or remembering your own painful experiences. Instead try just being with the person who needs comfort and let them know that you're right there with them. These difficult times are a precious opportunity for a different kind of relationship, a special experience of love.

The Buddhist concept of the "bodhisattva" is someone whose

life is devoted to service. We don't all think of oursselves in this way, but we all care deeply about the wellbeing of those we love, and most of us envision and wish for positive change for the world.

Pema Chodron, an American Buddhist teacher, says that bodhisattvas are *"those spiritual warriors who long to alleviate suffering, their own and that of others."* On this path she recommends we *"learn to use whatever pain or fear we experience to open our hearts to other people's distress."*

This intense desire to help reduce suffering is called bodhichitta, or awakened heart. It is, she says, *"the heartfelt yearning to free oneself from the pain of ignorance and habitual patterns in order to help others do the same. This longing to alleviate the suffering of others is the main point." And, she says, there's "no time to lose."*

Learning to face the reality of illness and death and suffering requires a kind of strength and courage, an open-heartedness and a willingness to face what Buddhists call the "full catastrophe" that can grow in us through the practice of Loving Presence.

With Patients or Clients

(for doctors, nurses,
mental health care providers, caregivers, etc.)

*In the ideal doctor/patient relationship, who is healed,
what is healed, and how the healing takes place
is often beyond understanding.*

~ Paul Brenner, MD

DOCTORS, NURSES, AND OTHERS in the caring professions are at high risk for burnout. Sometimes having "good bedside manner," is very difficult for any number of reasons, and finding the balance between holding appropriate professional distance and providing compassion and a calm, caring presence, is a challenge.

In May of 2018 in an article titled: "Why AI Will Never Beat a Good Doctor," Dr. David Rakel, author of *The Compassionate Connection: The Healing Power of Empathy and Mindful Listening,* and professor and chair of the Department of Family & Community Medicine at the University of New Mexico, reports:

> In my own research, I have found that we have the astounding ability to help others in a way that prompts their healing from within. My colleagues and I studied the compassionate connection in primary care clinics at the University of Wisconsin. We taught doctors to interact with patients using techniques of deep listening and empathy. We found that those who rated

their doctors high in empathy recovered from the common cold a day faster with milder symptoms than those who didn't. This wasn't just feel-good therapy; patients who felt a connection produced increased levels of disease-fighting immune cells.

This is the ultimate power of a practice of Loving Presence. There are doctors and nurses and other medical practitioners who practice Loving Presence naturally and who already recognize that they are more effective when they bring this state of mind to their time with patients. What is often not realized is that a Loving Presence state of mind benefits not only the patient, but the practitioner as well. It offers an antidote to the frustration, overwhelm, burnout, and sense of helplessness that comes with this kind of work.

So how can those in a medical profession practice Loving Presence at work? The first step is to practice enough self-care to maintain a quality of relaxed vitality, which for people in caring professions can be very challenging. Focusing on caring for oneself can be difficult and might even feel selfish for those who work every day caring for others. Nevertheless it is very important, and is a gift to patients or clients. So, too, is learning some simple ways to let patients know that you truly see them, human to human.

First of all, rather than trying to reassure a patient by dismissing or minimizing their concerns, the best way to reassure someone is actually to acknowledge their concerns in a way that the patient can hear: "I really get that this is worrying you. It must be so scary—" (you should never say "but" so this point say "...and") "—we'll check everything to make sure that we're dealing with it in the most effective way." This lets patients/clients feel acknowledged and know that you empathize, that you understand their concerns. It means facing your own fears and limitations.

Secondly, your intent to focus on the innate strengths and beauty of spirit in each person who comes to you for care with mindfulness, empathy, and compassion not only helps them, but also fills you up as the caregiver, and helps reduce the risk of burnout and sustain your energy as a helper. Spending even five minutes in a silent mindfulness practice between patients, and reminding yourself to **search for inspiration** in each patient in order to see the whole person, changes your state of mind and transforms your relationship with patients.

Of course it's true that there are sometimes things you need to do. And yet Loving Presence, in spite of being quiet, and often patiently inactive, provides the best context for a healthy human interaction, and for positive emotional change and healing to occur. The quality of your attention might have far more impact on others than anything you actually ***do.***

Within a Group

MANY OF US ARE PART OF A GROUP OF SOME TYPE. It might a group with a focus on providing support to people in recovery, people who live with mental illness, people who love someone with mental illness or substance abuse issues, or it might be a therapy group. It might focus on a creative pursuit like writing or crafting, it could be a book group, or a group focused on activism, education, spirituality, or any other situation in which people come together regularly (in person or virtually) to connect and speak honestly about their concerns.

Twelve Step groups provide support for millions of people in recovery from substance abuse issues. There are countless writing groups, many of them inspired by Natalie Goldberg's book, *Writing Down the Bones,* which brings mindfulness to writing practice. There are book groups and knitting groups and quilting groups and group psychotherapy. At first glance some of these groups might not seem likely places to introduce Loving Presence, but any time people come together with a shared focus offers an opportunity to connect with compassion and sincerity about the real issues in their lives.

Princeton sociologist Robert Wuthnow has researched the efficacy of small groups, especially to heal relationships. In an article in *Spirituality and Health* (Summer 2001) he wrote that 35% of adult Americans are involved in some kind of small group, and of these, 64% attend group meetings weekly. He says, "One of the most helpful aspects of the group process is being able to gain new perspective on one's own experiences by viewing them through others' eyes."

No matter what kind of group it is, we only feel safe to ask for help when we know we will be met with welcome and acceptance. Support groups ideally provide mirroring and understanding that nurtures the spirit and encourages us to make new, more creative choices in place of old, self-destructive behaviors. In a caring community of people who see through our defenses and recognize the vulnerability and the beauty within each of us, we can risk showing up as we are. Introducing the practice of Loving Presence and spending even a little time with it at the beginning of any gathering will magically transform the group experience for everyone.

In an article in Roberta Conlan's *States of Mind,* Esther Sternberg writes, "Just as studies show that stress tends to blunt the body's immune responses, making us more susceptible to infection and disease, research also shows that a supportive social environment or group therapy, by reducing stress hormone levels, can enhance immune response, including resistance to such diseases as cancer."

And Jean Shinoda Bolen, in her book ***The Millionth Circle: How to Change Ourselves and the World – The Essential Guide to Women's Circles,*** proposes that groups, and women's groups in particular, can have a ***ripple effect***—something like a hundredth monkey phenomenon. The idea is that when there are enough of these groups functioning in a certain way, they will change the world. "As we begin to change our personal relationships... It's like throwing pebbles in a pond; each one has an impact and an effect, with concentric rings of change rippling out and affecting other relationships."

Certainly, a healthy support group changes the world of the people in it, not only as a community, but in each person's other relationships as well. We have found this over and over with the groups of people who come together, even for a few days, to practice Loving Presence. Often the group itself becomes a healing community as well as a place of learning for the participants. At the very least, people go back to their relationships and families and to whatever communities they live and work in with an enhanced capacity to be present with the people in their lives. The effects ripple out and continue long after the group experience has ended.

There is certainly a great need now for better communication for peaceful relationships—in families and communities, as well as globally. Anything we can do to improve the way we treat ourselves and other people helps make the world a better place to live. The practice of Loving Presence in groups leads to Peacemaking.

Peacemaking

If we are peaceful... everyone in our family,
our entire society, will benefit from our peace.

~ Thich Nhat Hanh

IT HAS OFTEN BEEN SAID that peace in the world begins with inner peace. In truth, peacemaking involves a state of mind and a set of behaviors that affect us internally when expressed outwardly, and vice versa. Inner and outer become one and the same.

Loving Presence, and the peacemaking that results from this practice, is based on a conscious intention to act with authenticity and kindness, to create harmony instead of conflict, to be more responsive than reactive, to contribute to peaceful relations - at home and in the world. The best way to begin the intentional practice that results in peacemaking, just as with Loving Presence, is to start where we are - to bring some awareness to our habits and attitudes, especially to our ways of relating to others. Most of us already have at least a little self-awareness and some capacity for this kind of self-reflection.

It takes practice, and is a *practice*, to pay attention this way to ourselves, to notice how different people affect us, to be aware of how we think about life, to be aware of our impulses and reactions. The more we can practice this, the less reactive we will be, less "on automatic." Only by knowing about our underlying assumptions will we begin to see things clearly, without the old filter of preconceived ideas and habitual expectations.

The ability to pause, to reflect, to consider all possibilities, lets us see through the surface of things; it gives us the chance to stop and question our reactions. When it comes to human relations, old habits of perception and thinking and reacting are the biggest roadblocks to relating peacefully.

There are steps we can take to bring more consciousness to how we perceive life, make meaning of things, respond, and relate to others. All of these steps can be done in a few seconds with practice: first noticing our automatic thoughts and impulses, then pausing and opening up a space to look more deeply, perhaps to see things differently. At first we might need to do this in our imagination, as a post-situation fantasy done in retrospect, imagining possibilities for responding that have not yet become spontaneous. The practice is worthwhile. It eventually makes us less reactive, more creative in how we respond to others in a variety of life situations.

One new possibility that becomes available in human interactions when we can pause and notice the impulse to react (and choose to respond instead), is to look for, to search for, what it is about the other that is a reflection of us. We want to begin to see the ways we are similar to others, and they to us. Looking for and finding what's in common - instead of focusing only on the differences - is one of the keys to having more peaceful relations with others.

In his book, *Social Intelligence,* Daniel Goleman points out that most of the world's problems and conflicts arise from *"us and them"* thinking. We are much more likely to reject others who seem different from us, and to engage in conflict with *them*—whoever *they* are! Beginning to change the prejudices and biases that result in unnecessary conflict, and even war, means being willing to relate to others – to "them" – until we understand how we're all the same. Various projects have shown that when individuals from different groups have a chance to get to know each other, and to relate in a friendly way, it transforms old attitudes and prejudices towards whole groups.

When we can transcend the concept of "us" and "them", we take a huge step toward peacemaking in our world. Recognizing our own prejudices is essential. The next step is to let ourselves be inspired... to search for inspiration in the other. We want to look for what we can appreciate about other people, not necessarily to *like,* but at least to respect or admire. It's there in everyone.

When we allow others to evoke feelings of appreciation or inspiration in us, then we need to digest this appreciation and let it nourish us. Any response that comes from this state of mind is likely to lead to more peaceful relations. Any response that occurs after a pause—a pause for self-reflection, to feel appreciation, and to allow for different choices of how to respond—will not be just a repeat of old reactions. We are no longer on automatic when we practice this kind of self-reflection and new way of seeing others. A world of creative possibilities begins to open up for us and for those we relate to in our lives.

The practice of Peacemaking, as with Loving Presence, starts first of all by paying attention to yourself and to develop a habit of self-reflection. The basic steps are clear:

- Take a moment for *self-reflection:* notice what is happening for you internally. Let go of asking questions or interpreting. Listen without deciding. Let go of preconceived ideas, assumptions, and prejudices,

- Pause: take a moment to observe what is happening in the present moment. Breathe, *open a space* to reflect on your impulses,

- Experiment with a different way of seeing: *change your lens;* make way for a new or different way of perceiving,

- *Appreciate something* about the other person: what do you appreciate about the person or people you are with? What inspires you about them? Be curious about what you have in common. This invites Loving Presence.

- *Respond with empathy* rather than reacting automatically and habitually: notice first what is *called up* and then what is *called for*. This is the difference between a reaction and a response.

- *Be creative* about other possibilities; risk doing it differently. Consider that there are many options for responding (including no response). Allow for thoughts, images, intuition, memories, to show you the way.

Practicing these skills in a group setting allows for the possibility of relating more and more peacefully with others. This creates an opportunity to observe our automatic reactions to different kinds of triggers. We can assist each other on a journey of self-reflection and healing with this practice of Loving Presence. This work is an invitation to loving relationships and peacemaking.

A group can develop into a kind of sangha, a community in which people feel safer, supported, understood, welcome, belonging, appreciated, and loved—a community in which there is the chance to share discoveries with others, and to do so in ways that contribute to experiences based on kindness, authenticity, and peace. This means developing skillfulness in noticing our own and others' reactions, and learning to respond to them in ways that invite greater and greater levels of self-honesty, participation, and compassion for ourselves, as well as for others in community.

The whole process can be explored experientially, with a focus on taking our growing self-awareness into the kind of understanding of others that opens the heart of compassion and the door to peaceful relations within a group context. We can learn to relate to others in a way that cultivates safety wherever we are and in whatever group we find ourselves, including the global community.

As we become more deeply connected to ourselves, and to others around us, perhaps we may be able to reach our vision for a peaceful, sustainable world. Peacemaking based on the practice of Loving Presence requires a set of understandings and behaviors that affect us internally when expressed outwardly and vice versa. To maintain consciousness is to develop a capacity for self-reflection and witnessing which we bring to ourselves, our relationships, into organizations and society, and to the world. We move from learning how to calm our minds and open our hearts to becoming more compassionately aware of ourselves and others, to holding a calm and appreciative attitude toward others and to all life.

Loving Presence with Yourself

"Be what you are:
intelligence and love in action."

~ Nisargadatta Maharaj

IT IS SOMETIMES SAID THAT YOU CANNOT LOVE OTHERS until you can love yourself. Perhaps the opposite is true. You might find that the practice of Loving Presence with others is actually the best preparation for learning to be more loving, kind, and compassionate with yourself.

Perhaps there is a part of you that is judgmental and critical of yourself, a part that gets impatient or frustrated when you are not feeling successful or lovable. Your first awareness of this tendency might actually increase your self-judgment: "There I go again, being hard on myself; I'm so terrible at loving myself!" Recognizing this habit, then interrupting it to look instead for something you appreciate, just as you do in the practice of Loving Presence with others, begins to change this old pattern and make way for something new and positive.

Noticing how you can change the way you feel about others by how you see them, by how you choose to look at them, you learn to interrupt the ways of looking and thinking that make you feel critical, that disrupt your sense of inner peace, that interfere with feeling appreciation for others and for yourself. This paves the way for opening your heart and having more peaceful relationships everywhere, including with yourself.

When you can notice and interrupt old habits of self-criticism or self-rejection, you begin to change the quality of both your inner and outer relationships and to transform into a more loving expression of the spirit of who you truly are. You will discover that you *are* Loving Presence.

PRACTICE GUIDE

*Kathleen Raine, a Scottish poet, says that
unless you see a thing in the light of love,
you do not see it at all.
Love is the light in which we see light.
Love is the light in which we see each thing
in its true origin, nature, and destiny.
If we could look at the world in a loving way,
then the world would rise up before us
full of invitation, possibility, and depth."*

~ quoted by John O'Donohue
in *Anam Cara*

About these Practices

MANY OF THE PRACTICES HERE INVITE YOU to have a certain intention. Remember that they serve, more than anything else, as self reflection opportunities. As Moshe Feldenkrais used to say, *"You cannot do what you want until you know what you are already doing."*

So you may have an intention, for example, to be loving with someone, but what gets in your way? What are the habits that interfere with a natural loving state? You might wish to quiet your mind. But what are the mental habits that create the noise in your mind? You might have an intention to listen open-heartedly and you begin a conversation with this intention. But what habits of listening and reacting show up to cloud the space and perhaps even close your heart and mind?

Whatever intentional practice we suggest, such as **Listen without Deciding** for example, the real point is to watch what else happens and to learn about yourself, about your "unbearable automaticity" (Bargh and Chartrand, 1999).

Only when your habits come into conscious awareness is it possible to interrupt them and make other choices. Otherwise you are always reacting, rather than responding—you are driven by what's **called up,** rather than what's **called for.**

Here follows the instructions for the key practices already

described, as well as some complementary practices that can also be used to cultivate new habits of self-awareness, spaciousness, perceptual wisdom, seeing what's right, and especially, Loving Presence...

Mindfulness

THE ESSENCE OF MINDFULNESS is to be fully present to your experience, whatever it is: your thoughts, images, memories, breathing, body sensations, the sounds and smells and tastes, moods and feelings and the quality of your experience as a whole, as well as of the various parts. Mindfulness is the foundation for all the other practices that lead to Loving Presence. It is recommended as a daily practice and need only take a few minutes at a time. It is a kind of meditation practice and is possible for even small children to learn.

- Begin in a comfortable position. You want to be comfortable enough to feel relaxed without falling asleep.

- With eyes open or closed, begin to notice aspects of your present moment sensory experience whatever it is. For example, listen to the sounds around you.

- Become aware of your own breathing, but without trying to change it.

- Continue to let your attention include other physical sensations. What are you aware of happening in your body?

- Begin to include other aspects of your experience: thoughts, images, feelings, impulses. There is nothing more to do besides noticing your moment to moment experience.

Being With

- In pairs, sit silently facing your partner; get settled and mindful. Each does this practice at your own pace.

- When you're ready, open your eyes and look at your partner. Their eyes may be open or closed.

- If you sense any changes in your experience, especially if there is discomfort, close your eyes and silently study what's happening inside you.

- When you're ready, settle yourself again and open your eyes. Notice whatever happens.

- Repeat this cycle as many times as you like for several minutes.

- After maybe about 5-10 minutes, agree to stop and discuss with your partner what happened for you. Tell each other about your own experience.

Leaning Toward and Away

THIS IS AN AMAZING WAY TO DISCOVER unconscious attitudes around being close to others. The first reaction you have reveals a belief, a translation of the meaning of the movement. What surprises you?

- Sit in pairs, facing each other. Decide who will be A and B.

- A starts with eyes closed for a moment and then opens them to look at B.

- At this point, B very slowly leans slightly toward A.

- A closes eyes again to observe what this subtle movement evokes.

- When ready, A opens eyes again at which point B leans slightly back and away. Again A closes eyes to be with whatever reaction, feelings, thoughts etc are evoked.

- Reverse roles and repeat the experiment. Then report and discuss your experiences.

Monkey Mind

THIS IS A PRACTICE OF MINDFULNESS ON THE BREATH and is a good demonstration of how your mind and thoughts tend to jump around like a monkey. It is also an example of the kind of practice where you have an intention (counting breaths) but you really want to be more interested in what else happens.

- This can be done by yourself anytime for just a few minutes. Simply notice and silently count each exhalation.

- If you lose count, begin again at one. Do this for awhile, and notice what kinds of thoughts take you away from your breath... what habits of mind interrupt your intention to simply be present with your breathing?

- If you do this with one or more partners, after a few minutes share your self observations and experiences with each other.

Groundlessness

THIS IS A WAY OF CREATING SPACIOUS MIND. It's like what happens sometimes when you are traveling and have a moment when you wake up and can't remember where you are! What if you could invite such moments and stretch them out a little... open to mystery and the space of not knowing...?

- In pairs, one person becomes mindful and indicates when ready for a question.

- Your partner asks you a simple ordinary question such as "How old are you?" Or "Where's home? "What is your name?" "Who are your parents?"

- Silently notice the automatic answer that pops up right away, but then wait to find a place of really not knowing or at least not knowing for sure. Can you be unattached to your answers?

- Stay with this state of not knowing for awhile to get the embodied feeling of it...

- When you are ready for another question, say aloud, "I don't know." Your partner then asks another question like this. Keep the questions simple.

- If you really cannot find a place of not knowing to one or more questions, just say "Pass."

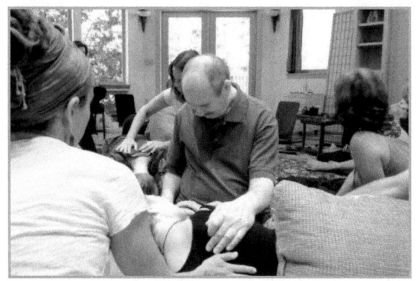

Ron Kurtz working in session.

- Continue this way until you have heard several questions and experienced a place of not knowing at least once and observed what happens... what is your embodied experience of not knowing?

- Reverse roles and repeat the exercise. Then discuss the experience.

Listen Without Deciding

THIS IS ANOTHER EXAMPLE OF A SELF STUDY PRACTICE that starts with an intention as an experiment. Here you will have an opportunity to notice the kinds of decisions and assumptions that are listening habits, even when you intend to listen with an open mind.

- In pairs, or a small group, one person talks for a few minutes about a recent experience.

- As listener, have the intention to simply listen without deciding anything. The success of this practice is not about being able to listen without deciding anything, but rather to discover and later discuss some of your mental listening habits.

- Let everyone have a chance to listen this way and then report (confess!) what each of you noticed about yourselves.

Seeing and Being Seen

IN ORDER TO BE REALLY AND RADICALLY PRESENT with another, it's important to recognize attitudes about seeing or looking at someone, and feelings about being seen. This can be done by yourself anytime for just a few minutes. Simply notice and silently count each exhalation.

- Sit with a partner facing one another. Close your eyes and turn your attention to your present moment experience to begin with so you will more easily notice if your experience changes.

- When you are ready, open your eyes to look at each other. Have someone slowly say a few statements to you about seeing and being seen: "It's safe to be seen." "It's okay to really see someone."

- You might want to close your eyes after each statement to mindfully observe your experience.

- After listening to the statements this way and noticing what happens for you, report and discuss your experience. Was there one statement in particular that you felt a reaction to? What did you discover about old ideas and habits around seeing and being seen?

Blink

THERE ARE LOTS OF VARIATIONS OF THE BLINK EXERCISE. It's another way of seeing that can bypass the rational mind. Use a *blink* anytime you are looking at someone else to allow for another kind of perception and perhaps give you a chance to see or imagine something about the person that is more subtle, less obvious. Always remember that any observation might reveal more about you than about the other person.

This practice can be done with people sitting or standing together in pairs, or in small groups one person at a time being observed by the partners who begin with eyes closed and then simply open and shut their eyes for a split second to get a quick impression rather than taking a good look.

- One frame to suggest for the blinkers that when you open your eyes, you'll see someone who's just come to your front door. Notice what impression you get. Who is this person and what are they doing at your door?

- Or another blink: open your eyes just for a second and get a glimpse as if you're seeing someone standing in a schoolyard. How old are they? What are they doing? How are they feeling?

Who Do You See? (A Larger Self)

THIS CAN BE DONE IN A GROUP SETTING, or anywhere. You can do it sitting in a coffee shop or on a bus or in an airport, anywhere there are people you can silently observe...

First close your eyes and imagine that when you look around, everyone you see will be one of these:

- Someone who has saved someone else's life,

- Someone who has written a book,

- Someone who just got out of hospital,

- Someone just nominated for a Nobel Prize,

- A five year old...!

With each frame, how do you see differently? What qualities are apparent with each? How does your embodied experience change a little (or a lot!) with each perception?

Seeing Through

THIS PRACTICE IS DONE IN PAIRS OR SMALL GROUPS. Each person has a turn to be observed this way. Remember that your observations may be more about you than about the person you're observing. It's also a good opportunity to discern the difference between your observations and your impressions. There is more safety in reporting them with this understanding.

- First one person just sits or stands while you, the partners, blink them—opening your eyes just long enough (a split second) for an impression to register. It might be a surprising impression, like a quality or an image of another person or of a different situation.

- Next the person can recite something like a simple nursery rhyme: "Mary had a little lamb/ its fleece was white as snow/ and everywhere that Mary went/ the lamb was sure to go." Here you might get an impression of the person as a child.

- Then the person will get up, walk away about five or ten steps, pick up an imaginary or real object, and return to their place. Observers, notice how they seem to do this.

- Finally the person can say a significant statement twice: once with their eyes open, then again with eyes closed. For example, this can be a statement of what is important to them at this moment in their life, or something personal that they think is not obvious to others. Often a different impression is created when the person speaks with their eyes closed than with eyes open.

- After all these observations, the partners can report their experiences and tell the person about whatever they imagined based on their observations and impressions. (Remember that you may observe the person's breathing change and you might imagine what they are feeling. The first is an observation and the second is an impression. Report them this way if possible.)

Walking Toward

LIKE THE **LEANING TOWARD** EXPERIMENT, this is a way to discover something about your unconscious interpretations of others' movements and intentions. Your automatic reactions happen before your rational mind tells you what is going on and these reactions usually have more to do with your past than with present time.

As a Buddhist teacher once told me, in the first moment buddhas and all sentient beings are alike. A buddha is someone who is awake. Until we wake up, we are on automatic. We can stay unconscious and hang onto our reactions and assumptions, or we can wake up to the moment as it is and interrupt our reactions so they don't last as long or get as intense. But they still happen. Again, the almost unbearable automaticity of being!

Practice **Walking Toward** with one or more partners. In pairs, a third person might assist by observing.

- One person simply stands still while a partner slowly walks toward you from several feet away.

- You can slow them down or stop their approach simply with a hand gesture or closing your eyes to observe your experience.

- Continue until the partner is close enough to have a little discussion. Of course, the partner walking toward you is

119

having an experience also and needs to be curious about themselves.

- Reverse roles when you are ready.

- Another variation to follow the Walking Toward practice involves doing the same thing, but both the partner walking toward and the person being approached have the intention to imagine that the other person has a gift for them. This might be an actual tangible present or a more spiritual kind of gift. How does this alter the experience of the relationship?

Priming the Pump

THIS PRACTICE IS A SIMPLE WAY FOR PEOPLE IN A GROUP
to share something personal that primes the pump for Loving
Presence.

- Get together with one or more others to recall and talk
  about someone in your life who you think of as a blessing…
  perhaps someone who made a difference in your childhood
  or someone you love or admire. It might be someone you
  know personally, or a person you've read about that has
  been an inspiration. Take a few minutes each to talk about
  how this person has been important for you.

- When you're listening to each other, there's no need to
  ask questions or say anything. Simply listen with all your
  attention and with your heart open to hear and feel the
  impact of the person's story.

- After this sharing, spend a few minutes talking about how
  this sharing felt… notice and report how you feel now,
  individually and together.

Search for Inspiration and Nourishment

THIS IS A WAY TO PRACTICE LISTENING and being with in an open and receptive way that nourishes everyone.

- In pairs or small groups, one person at a time talks about something personally meaningful.

- Listeners, listen in silence and simply let yourselves be inspired, touched, and nourished in some deep way by this experience of listening to and being with this person.

- After the person finishes talking, briefly discuss what this experience was like for each or all of you. What was it like to listen this way... to be listened to in this way?

- Let each person have a turn being the talker and being a listener.

Being With 1-2-3

LIKE THE **BEING WITH** PRACTICE, this is done in pairs facing each other, and invites three different kinds of experiences with a simple change of lens.

- Each person alternates between eyes closed and eyes open at your own pace.

- Move through three different stages of looking at your partner and notice how each frame or lens might change your embodied experience.

- First, simply look and notice your automatic reactions of seeing and being seen.

- Second, remind yourself that this person has probably had some challenges and losses in their life. Have the intention to look for signs of present or past pain or suffering. Notice what you see and what you imagine, and then observe your experience with these impressions.

- Finally, remember that this person has survived whatever difficulties life has given them. Intentionally search for signs of strengths, or impressions of qualities that inspire you. Notice what your experience is with these observations and impressions.

- Tell each other about your experience as you moved through these three frames.

Hand on the Back

THIS IS A LOVELY WAY TO CONNECT AND SUPPORT EACH other to discover any unconscious reactions to touch. It is done with respect and curiosity and deep permission.

- In pairs, one person, take a moment in mindfulness to imagine where a hand placed on your back would feel good.

- Tell your partner where you'd like them to put one or both of their hands, somewhere on your back. As they do this, notice if it feels good or if a small adjustment would feel better. Take the time to make the adjustments until this touch feels right. Then, simply enjoy the feeling of it for a few minutes.

- Your partner will wait to allow you to just enjoy having their hand on your back, perhaps noticing when your breathing seem to relax or just intuitively deciding on the timing for the next step...

- Your partner softly asks this question. "What does this hand seem to be saying to you?"

- When you hear the question, don't try to come up with an answer. Simply notice whatever happens in your experience. You might have a verbal answer emerge. You might have a memory or a feeling or a shift in something else you're noticing... Wait and see what happens spontaneously.

- When you're ready, turn to your partner and tell them about your experience. Then reverse roles.

Intimacy

IN PAIRS, SPEND 5-10 MINUTES DOING THIS before having a regular conversation. Wait till afterward to tell each other about your experience. First have a simple dialogue but follow these rules:

- As much as possible maintain eye contact with each other,

- Take turns speaking only about your present experience in one or two statements at a time,

- Avoid interrupting each other.

Loving Presence

HERE IS THE ULTIMATE LOVING PRESENCE PRACTICE.

- In pairs, or in a small group, one person talks about something personal. Remind the talker to look at their listeners from time to time at least.

- Partner/listener: search for sources of nourishment and inspiration in the talker, not in the content of what they are saying. Listen without making any interventions.

- Partner/listener: notice and inhibit your impulses to do or say anything else. Listen silently.

- Finally, discuss your experience (not the issue the person was talking about). Just talk about the experience of loving presence and how it affected you, whether as the listener or as the talker.

And finally,

Before You Speak

- There is one talker and one or more listeners; the talker talks about something important.

- Listener, before any intervention, wait for the talker's signal that it is your turn; before you say anything, do three things first:

    1. Notice something that feels nourishing or inspiring.

    2. Name this silently to yourself.

    3. Appreciate it in silence for a moment or longer.

- Finally, respond in a way that feels natural and easy. Let a spontaneous response arise from your Loving Presence state of mind.

- After a while talk about your experience with each other.

I Take Refuge

~ *Ron Kurtz*
September 15, 2001
The day of his marriage to Terry Toth.

I Take Refuge in all Buddhas in Sangha
in Dharma
in my body and yours
Meher Baba, Swami Rama, the ones I've known
the ones I never met
the holy ones
the sweet, laughing ones
the beautiful ones
who found love,
in this house of pain.

I take refuge this terrible day,
in poets, music makers dancers, dancing freedom
of the body and the mind
in all seekers
who broke the iron hold
of separation
all lovers... young ones, still surprised,
old ones who know love's sad sweetness

Ron Kurtz and wife, Terry Toth

I take refuge this beautiful day in my loved ones
wife, child, friends,
students, colleagues
in the holy ones
all the holy, precious
keepers.
in hearts that break
open, that rise up
to comfort, defend, protect

I take refuge in all of these
in the old wisdom,
they who found it, sung it
the laws, how it all works

Not only refuge, I take sustenance and Hope,
for peace in every heart
in my body and yours
for peace in every mind

for wisdom to see through
our pain, all pain, pain
which drops us blind,
fearful, angry, down
 into a deep well
of nothing but self and self-
concern, burning with
greed and desperation.

from all of this, I take refuge...
in the law, the teachings,
the good books,
the holy writings
of Buddhas, saints,
preachers, drunk on love,
all who saw clearly
saw and sang, the good news, gospel, dharma,
going from
mind to mind, soul to soul
touching so many, touching
the seekers holding hands
standing together, joyous, celebrating buoyant,
even as time flows
people flashing by,
faces in a dream

I take refuge in you,
sweet friend, stranger,
in you and me
as one being.

References/Bibliography

Bargh and Chartrand, Tanya (1999). "The Unbearable Automaticity of Being." *American Psychologist: Vol. 54, No. 7,* 462-479.

Batchelor, S. (1998). *Buddhism Without Beliefs: A Contemporary Guide to Awakening.* Riverhead.

Betti, Ugo (1956) *Three Plays,* translated by Henry Reed. Grove Press.

Bolen, Jean Shinoda (1999). *The Millionth Circle: How to Change Ourselves and The World–The Essential Guide to Women's Circles.* Conari Press.

Brazier, David (1998). *The Feeling Buddha: A Buddhist Psychology of Character, Adversity and Passion.* Fromm Intl.

Chödrön, Pema (2005). *No Time to Lose: A Timely Guide to the Way of the Bodhisattva.* Shambhala.

Crow, David (2001). *In Search of the Medicine Buddha: A Himalayan Journey.* Jeremy P. Tarcher/Putnam.

Depraz, N., Varela, F.J. and Vermersch, P. (1999). *Investigating Phenomenal Consciousness,* edited by M.Velman. Benjamin Publishers, Amsterdam.

Eliot, T.S. "The Love Song of J. Alfred Prufrock" *Collected Poems 1909-1962.* Houghton Mifflin Harcourt. Available from https://www.poetryfoundation.org/poetrymagazine/poems/44212/the-love-song-of-j-alfred-prufrock. Accessed

August 29, 2019.

Foster, Jeff. "Do not try to open your heart." Available from https://
www.facebook.com/LifeWithoutACentre/posts/22400530
59425623 Accessed August 29, 2019.

Goleman, Daniel (1995). *Emotional Intelligence: Why It Can
Matter More Than IQ.* Bantam.

Goleman, Daniel (2006). *Social Intelligence: The New Science of
Human Relationships.* Bantam.

Hesse, Herman (1922). *Siddhartha.* New Directions: 1951.

Hubble, M.A., Duncan, B.L. and Miller, S.D. (1999). *The Heart
and Soul of Change: What Works in Therapy.* American
Psychological Association.

Kurtz, Ron (2018). *The Hakomi Way: Consciousness & Healing.*
Stone's Throw Publications.

Lewis, T., Amini, F. and Lannon, R. (2001). *A General Theory of
Love.* Vintage Books.

Maharaj, Sri Nisargadatta. *I Am That.* Full text available at: https://
archive.org/stream/IAmThatBySriNisargadattaMaharaj/I-
Am-That-by-Sri-Nisargadatta-Maharaj_djvu.txt Accessed August 30, 2019

Mahoney, Michael (1991). *Human Change Processes* Basic Books.

Nyanaponika Thera (2001). *The Power of Mindfulness (Mindfulness
Series 3).* Original publication, 1802. Buddha Dharma Education
Association Inc. available at: http://www.buddhanet.net/pdf_
file/powermindfulness.pdf Accessed August 30, 2019

O'Donohue, John (1998). *Anam Cara: A Book of Celtic Wisdom.*
Harper Perennial.

Palmer, Helen. *The Enneagram: Understanding Yourself and the
Others in Your Life.* San Francisco: Harper Collins, 1988. pp.
4-9, 12-15.

Rakel, David (2018). *The Compassionate Connection: The Healing Power of Empathy and Mindful Listening.* W. W. Norton & Company.

Rakel, David and Golant, Susan (2018) "Bedside manner matters: Why AI will never beat a good doctor." Available from https://www.salon.com/2018/05/13/bedside-manner-matters-why-ai-will-never-beat-a-good-doctor/ Accessed August 31, 2019

Ramachandran, V.S. and Blakeslee, Sandra (1999). *Phantoms in the Brain: Probing the Mysteries of the Human Mind.* William Morrow.

Rumi, Jelaluddin."Each Note" from *Say I Am You: Poetry Interspersed with Stories of Rumi and Shams,* translated by John Moyne and Coleman Barks. Maypop: 1994.

Salzberg, Sharon (2008). *Loving-Kindness: The Revolutionary Art of Happiness.* Shambhala.

Sheldrake, Rupert (1994). *Seven Experiments That Could Change the World: A Do-It-Yourself Guide to Revolutionary Science.* Fourth Estate Ltd.

Siegel, Daniel (2001). *The Developing Mind: How Relationships and the Brain Interact to Shape Who We Are.* The Guilford Press.

Siegel, D. and Hartzell, M. (2013). *Parenting from the Inside Out: How a Deeper Self-Understanding Can Help You Raise Children Who Thrive.* TarcherPerigee.

Sternberg, Esther (1999). "Emotions and Disease: A Balance of Molecules" in *States of Mind: New Discoveries About How Our Brains Make Us Who We Are,* edited by Roberta Colman. Wiley.

Strupp, H. H., & Hadley, S. W. (1979). "Specific vs nonspecific factors in psychotherapy: A controlled study of outcome." *Archives of General Psychiatry, 36(10),* 1125-1136.

Thurman, Robert (1998). *Inner Revolution: Life, Liberty, and the Pursuit of Real Happiness.* Riverhead.

Wagamese, Richard (2016). *Embers.* Douglas and McIntyre.

Weil, Simone (1942) "Reflections on the Right Use of School Studies with a View to the Love of God." *Waiting for God.* HarperCollins: 2009, 57–65.

White, Kenneth (1980). "The Loveliness is Everywhere." from *A Walk Along The Shore.* Le Nouveau Commerce.

Wilson, Timothy (2002). *Strangers to Ourselves: Discovering the Adaptive Unconscious.* Belknap Press.

Wuthnow, Robert (2001). "The Power of a Few," *Spirituality and Health (Summer 2001),* 47-49. Available from https://spiritualityhealth.com/articles/2001/06/01/the-power-of-a-few-to-help-lighten-your-load. Accessed August 31, 2019

About Donna Martin

DONNA MARTIN, M.A. is an international Hakomi Trainer who lives in Canada and has taught all over the world. Donna worked closely with Ron Kurtz for the last twenty years of his life.

Donna has been a yoga teacher since the 70's and first met Ron Kurtz at a retreat center in Canada called Hollyhock where she was teaching yoga and he was teaching Hakomi. Both had been influenced by the Feldenkrais method and by Buddhism, and they instantly recognized a similarity in their styles. Donna worked closely with Ron during the development of his "refined" version of Hakomi and the Practice of Loving Presence. She and Ron worked on the material for this book for several years before his death in 2011 and taught this approach to thousands of people around the world.

Donna also has an MP3 guiding the key loving presence practices. This is available on www.hakomi.ca and www. reflectivepresence.com.

Printed in the USA
CPSIA information can be obtained
at www.ICGtesting.com
LVHW020740251023
761901LV00008B/252